Common Sense and Whiskey

Common Sense and Whiskey

Modest Adventures Far from Home

Bill Murray

Bhutan, Borneo, Burma, Greenland, Guangxi, Lake Baikal, Madagascar, Malawi, Papua New Guinea, Paraguay, Patagonia, Southern Caucasus, Trans-Siberian Railroad, Sri Lanka, Tibet

•••••

EP

EarthPhotos Books
Young Harris, Georgia USA • 2011

Common Sense and Whiskey
Modest Adventures Far from Home

Because of the dynamic nature of the internet, some of the web sites mentioned in this book may have changed or no longer be valid.

Photographs in this book are available for purchase or download from, and appear in color on, the web site EarthPhotos.com.

Printed in the United States of America.

ISBN-13: 978-0615467313
ISBN-10: 0615467318

Cover Photographs: Negombo Beach, Sri Lanka & near Dali, rural China

Visit these associated web sites:
CommonSenseAndWhiskey.com
EarthPhotos.com

·····

EarthPhotos Books
4625 Murray Lane
Young Harris, GA 30582 USA
www.earthphotos.com
800.229.2046
706.379.0675

·····

Neophyte Publishing
2011

For my father, William J. Murray

CONTENTS

● ● ● ● ●

FOREWORD

A long time ago, when there were still independent bookstores, I found some little tour books about Soviet cities - Leningrad, Moscow, Kiev - published by the Novosti Press in Moscow. I still have them today.

When I see a travel guide to an offbeat location like Yemen, say, or Gabon, I buy it without even opening the cover. Far away places are just plain alluring, and the more exotic the better.

But beyond the guidebook, how to find out about them?

Lots of travel books detail the author's vast, grimly accumulated knowledge of this or that historical oddity, and sometimes that's only tenuously connected to the traveling that's actually being done.

Lengthy examinations of 14th century funerary rites in Assam or the surprising mating rituals of arboreal reptiles can grow tedious. I'm pretty sure that's not just me.

Some personal stories on the internet are great. But some of the stuff - really, nobody cares what Phil and Jenny paid for every hotel room in Andalusia (converted to dollars, every penny). And nobody wants to read the loving list of each dish at every meal Mr. And Mrs. Kincaid enjoyed on this, their seventh trip to Kerala.

I want to know what I'd find if I hopped on a plane and went there and tried to negotiate my way around. What does it feel like to drive around the place?

•••••

Jeffrey Tayler says that to stay young, we need novelty in regular doses. My beautiful and intrepid wife Mirja (who isn't intimidated by anything that I know of) and I have had just that, in odd corners of the planet from Greenland to Madagascar to Papua New Guinea to Albania just after it threw off totalitarianism.

Robert Louis Stevenson wrote, "For my part, I travel not to go anywhere, but to go. I travel for travel's sake. The great affair is to move."

Colin Thubron said just about the same thing: "You go because you are still young and crave excitement, the crunch of your boots in the dust; you go because you are old and need to understand something before it's too late. You go to see what will happen."

I think they're both right. You just go.

These aren't stories steeped in minutiae, or complicated with detail. Some are more about the getting there than the destination. And I'm pretty sure everything here is unencumbered by ponderous history or unnecessary tram schedules.

- Bill Murray, Young Harris, Georgia, April, 2011

●●●●●

Photos from our travels, 17,570 as I write this, are on our web site, EarthPhotos.com. To see all the photos in this book in color, and more photos corresponding to each chapter, visit *A Common Sense and Whiskey Companion* at:

www.EarthPhotos.com/CSandW

1 LAKE BAIKAL, SIBERIA

Like always, the eastern shore of Lake Baikal, the Sacred Lake, the Pearl of Siberia, was shrouded in mist all the way up above the peaks. Out on the water, in the morning, the wind cast a determined late season chill.

The captain stood broad shouldered, square-faced and hale with a crew-cut and a Reebok jacket, and I liked him right away. Not a lick of English, but he made us coffee with water from a big painted teapot below decks and offered pelmeni that we coveted but politely refused. Couldn't be sure we wouldn't be eating his own lunch.

Over the weekend the jetty at Listvyanka, a bedraggled tourist town on the lake, had been packed with trinket vendors and mongers of exotic Siberian fish like omul and grayling. On Monday morning it stood deserted except for a drunken bottle recycler and three or four ships' mates and dockhands, loitering around stale cigarette butts and discarded wrappers.

The new week crept up in autumnal dampness, the clouds in stratified layers. Surveying the dock and our little ship, the Poruchik, the Gilligan's Island theme edged into my head. Ours was a four-hour tour – a simple west to east crossing of one of the world's great lakes.

The Poruchik, white, blue and red tricolor flapping above, was a diesel-burning forty-foot cruiser with two cabins below decks and a separate galley and mess. Must have started life as a fishing boat before they'd retrofitted it for charters, with benches, tables and chairs, and there were liqueurs and vodka and a TV below.

Pine forest stretched around rocky outcrops up the hills along shore. An hour after the Poruchik set sail, we came alongside a settlement called Bolshoi Koti, the last, tenuous human imprint, and then, north for miles of lakeshore, lonely primeval forest reigned.

For some time the Poruchik aimed for a promontory that wasn't on my map, and then swung hard to starboard for the crossing. A low blanket of gray from the west, from Irkutsk, replaced the sunshine of the last few days.

There were arrangements for later. Someone from Ulan Ude "will meet you at Kluevka (a place you are going to). This is definitely." Made it seem like the Russian Autonomous Republic of Buryatia was a foreign country, not simply the other side of the lake. And who knew, maybe it would be.

The temperature plunged when we swung away from the protection of shore and into open water, and after an hour and forty minutes, the mountains of the Ardaban Range on the far side of Baikal loomed tantalizingly close, breaking above the clouds.

Back home, imagining exotic Siberia, I naively thought it would be fun to "get out on the lake," like it would be fun to have a nice piece of candy. But out in its gray middle, Baikal slapped me humble, tossing and pounding the Poruchik to grab our attention and insist that it's a mighty inland sea. Finally, all you could do onboard was just hold on.

We ate a lunch of bread, tomatoes, sausage, cheese and onion down below, and wished we hadn't. We went out for air. When I went back down to clean up, bottles, plates and chairs littered the floor.

Eventually we made the eastern shore, and found our way into Ulan Ude with just enough time to walk to the parliament square before dark. Kids giggled at a massive Lenin head there. ("It looks really funny with snow on top.")

The hotel still employed Soviet-era floor ladies, whose job it was to mind your business. Ours drolly noted our extraordinary good fortune. Because of "environmental conference" with "important delegates" (the lobby buzzed with them), they'd turned on the hot water.

Silva's own hand, improbably, built the yellow plyboard breakfast and general headquarters shack where we warmed up over coffee. It perched on rocks some few meters from freezing, lapping water.

His sister Lilliana and her husband Filita were visiting from Florence, original Home of All Culture, and I suspect just maybe they considered Silva a bloody wide open, straight ahead idjit.

Loud and fifty, soft-hearted, quick to take a stand and quick to back away from it, Silva, with an impossibly full graying mustache and tousled hair, was a real piece of work, with eight bambinos - four in Italia and four in Ilulissat.

Silva shuffled across the kitchen, singing, whistling, posing, acting like supervising his sister Lilliana, who did all the cooking. What would he do when she went home to Italy?

Silva got caught up in the drama of the changing weather. We'd been there half an hour. Eyes widening, palms spread wide, he told us, "We cannot risk our lives to take you back if the weather is worse tomorrow!"

We sipped our coffee and watched him realize that since we'd just arrived he might be getting off on the wrong foot. He retreated behind his hand and allowed as how on the other hand his sister had to fly to Denmark on the same flight as us. When you can sit and watch a man think, his is a disarming guilelessness.

•••••

Mirja and I hiked up along a steep ridge to see the mouth of a glacier called Kangilerngata Sermia, forty speedboat minutes away. We traced the side of desolate Kangerdlo Bay to the north and scaled the western ridge to walk back along Lake Taserssuaq. Up on the ridge Mirja played with a bird, a tiny handful of brown that followed us just for the novelty.

Mirja set out to pick mushrooms. When she found a little brown-capped thing she declared, "Greenlandic people say there are no poisonous mushrooms in Greenland and I believe them. If I die in Greenland, it is my destiny," and she ate it and she didn't die.

The world felt constrained, all gray and closed in around the edges. We walked just several meters below the cloud line that hugged the mountain, kicking tiny, bell-shaped, yellow-rimmed flowers called lavender Lapland cassiope. Truth be known, this was more slog, slowed by bog and marsh, than wilderness adventure.

•••••

From the ridge you could see an old collapsed shack, fallen in on itself, from Ataa's trading post days.

"We keep it as a museum," Silva grinned.

The building next door had "119" painted on its roof. Before radar was sophisticated, the "119" marking helped U.S. pilots navigate on their way north to a DEWS (The Distant Early Warning System during the Cold War, set up to detect Soviet intercontinental ballistic missiles) base up north at Thule. It showed supply planes where to parachute in supplies.

•••••

We asked Silva for water to take on our hike and drew a stone-cold blank look of surprise. He rummaged around and came back with a bottle with Coca-Cola still rolling around inside it, and told us to take it down to the creek to wash it out and fill it up because the water here is completely clean.

When we left to hike up the hill, he promised us home cooked caribou for dinner and there sure was, caribou and potatoes and smoked halibut, whipped up by Lilliana and Filita, and it was outstanding.

A crowd of Germans had sailed in, and we had a rollicking good time in Greenlandic, English, German, Danish and Italian. Everybody understood a little bit of what everybody else said, and there was lively Italian style family cooking,

Silva and Lilliana humming and puttering and feeling at home.

Then came an astonishing knock at the door. We all sat up to welcome three people from a boat around the bay who needed petrol. Their boat was the Nosy Be and that perked up Mirja and me, because Nosy Be is a resort town in Madagascar. We've never been there, but some years ago a few thousand dollars were charged to our American Express card from a resort there.

•••••

Before the end of dinner, Silva developed a mischievous grin.

"Beeel, are you tired?"

"After eight beers and caribou I will be," I reckoned.

Silva grew reticent. "Then I will suggest nothing." But he couldn't contain himself and the next thing you knew we were tearing across the bay in a speedboat and Silva, behind the wheel, was screaming, "It's not coooollllldddd!"

It must've been 9:30, might have been ten. "Wanna see some seals?" he twinkled, and off we went, toward the mouth of a fjord called Kangerdluarssuk.

"How far is it over there, Silva?"

"Ten kilometers," he shouted. A waffling hand. "Twelve."

Glassy smooth, no chop, my thermometer read 46, but try sitting centimeters over water in air that's 46 degrees, tearing across the sea in Greenland at night. It's cold.

"We have to know the icebergs," Silva was shouting. "That one is sick ice. Cannot go close."

We trolled the coast and we didn't find any seals.

"We are worried," he told us with a twist of the mustache, maybe because he was a sage conservationist, maybe because his camp promised seal safaris.

After a good effort, Silva flat out raced back across the water, singing uproarious Italian nationalist songs then whistling Copland then humming a British march. There were no life vests. Just Silva, Mirja, me and the bare white bottom of the boat.

The south wind set in - an evil wind, pulling the wet up around the mountains behind Ataa, at the north end of the bay. Warmth whipped away on the wind.

•••••

Silva assigned us to a barracks with four rooms, each with bunk beds, a common room and a biological toilet. Nobody was there except us.

Silva came into the bunker around midnight. He would sleep there too. Eyes fired with the prospect of deals, earnestly, eye to eye, he told us of his plans for world kayak competitions and an international dive center right here, and ice golf in Iliminaq.

•••••

Greenland is to the Kingdom of Denmark as Tahiti is to France. There's considerable home rule, with a 27-seat parliament. Copenhagen is suzerain, maintains the courts and subsidizes prices. When we visited the only convenient access was via SAS from Copenhagen.

•••••

Approaching Greenland's gateway airport at Kangerlussuaq, you fly across mountains of rock, covered nearly to the top with snow. Nothing else. No people down there. As far as I saw, there wasn't a tree on the island. There were no highways. You got around by air, ferry or dog sled. There are only 55,000 people, and they all live around the coast.

Kangerlussuaq Airport is on the Canada side of the ice sheet on a coastal plain between bare hills alongside a sandy sluice that's also called Kangerlussuaq, or the long fjord, 105 miles from the sea. The ice cap is 17 miles east. Kangerlussuaq isn't a city. It's just the airport.

The oldest rocks anywhere are here - 3.7 billion years old where the earth is maybe 4.6 - and if you could get at the soil underneath the ice cap you'd find it (they think) 1.6 billion years old. They say the ice is so thick and heavy and it's been pressing on the center of the island so long that the interior may be up to 360 meters below sea level.

•••••

Northbound to Ilulissat, 250 kilometers above the Arctic Circle, we sat in a jam-packed DeHavilland including two seats of mail. For a time we weren't sure of getting seats.

"The mail," explained the ticket clerk, "has priority here."

Glacial lakes – tarns - skipped from the ice cap to the shore. Mineral laden fjords turned every shade of aqua, kelp, deep blue, almost brown. Mere meters separated deep, seductively dark blue tarns from sluicy gray, narrow channels that wound down to Baffin Bay.

Twenty-five minutes outside Ilulissat icebergs appeared offshore. Hard to tell how tall they were, hard to find a reference, and road number one was nowhere. I thought of the middle of the outback, just unedifying, useless land - here without brush, with icebergs instead.

•••••

None of Ilulissat had a plan. Built on an uneven, rocky promontory, it sprawled out of control (in a modest-sized way) not with roads so much as trails between boulders.

I was the only passenger on the bus into town, and finally the driver stopped, turned around and wondered, "Where you want to go?" I didn't know, so I popped out where we were, at Super 1 market.

You'd be surprised what you could buy there: Tomatoes, bags of mean little onions and dull potatoes, dill and one stout yellow melon. Withered yellow and red and green bell peppers, un-bought and forlorn, apparently didn't salve the Inuit palate.

• • • • •

The freighter Sophie Cristina, drowsy red, sat docked at the harbor. Massive, appalling heaps of trash lined the docks. Maybe it was just a collection problem. Maybe snow covered the stuff most of the time. But just now trash stood as high as the dumpsters along the waterfront.

I set out up the hill toward the glacier. Now this glacier, that presses from the ice cap down the fjord to the sea, is the most prolific calving glacier outside Antarctica. They'll nod earnestly over astounding statistics, like that the amount of water frozen in the ice that's pushed out into Disko Bay every day would supply New York City for a year. And the bergs loom over town, moving and shifting with the current, changing colors with the angle of the sun. It takes over an hour to sail across the mouth of the fjord.

I swore I heard gunshots. A lone fishing boat bobbed offshore. I sat on a rock and stared. It happened again, a couple times more. I couldn't make out whether the fisherman had a rifle and what was he doing anyway, shooting fish?

Turned out those were no gunshots. They were just oxygen under pressure, escaping from the ice. Happens all the time.

Up on the hills you'd hear the sled dogs. They'd yip, and the men were a whistlin' lot. Yippin' and whistlin' and poppin'.

• • • • •

translated. He had his own nearly identical house directly behind Namba.

Namba's son taught all the villagers how to weave the elaborate finials high above their doors, at the peak of the houses, too high to reach from the floor of the house, way above the ground - no idea how they did it.

Namba brought out the family's most prized possession, an old bridal veil made of thousands of tiny nassa shells. I tried it on, too flippantly. We handed it around and I held it too long. Lawrence, our guide, went full reverential.

"It is byoo-tee-ful!" he murmured.

I suggested it took weeks to weave.

"Months."

Namba walked us down to the ground and posed proudly on his front step leaning heavily on his cane, his ear lobes elongated in some traditional tribal thing, sporting a tattered orange Brisbane Broncos T-shirt, smiling a broad smile ruined by red stains of betel nut.

Lawrence told him we would mail him his picture. His pidgin said it would take "one moon."

Along the path from Namba's house, ancient pipe-smoking women sat weaving baskets. A social knot of men stood, advising how to carve a twelve foot communal table into a crocodile.

Two men did the actual work, rendering a recognizable creature from a solid block of wood using Swiss-made metal tools and hand-carved mallets. Maybe they found the tree back in the woods, or maybe they snared it floating down the river.

Two dugout canoes glided by as if on fire. They took along a clay pot, and when they caught a fish they smoked it right on the boat. The smoke kept away the nat nats.

• • • • •

In Arabia you must come in, sit down, drink Pepsi before negotiating can begin. In Tambanum they got right down to business. When a boat tied up they brought all their artifacts and laid 'em out on the riverbank. And they were too quick with their fallback position.

"How much?"

"Fifteen kina." Pause.

"Second price twelve kina."

They had no jobs. There were no jobs. They just hung in the village, 3000 in Tambanum, with no power, ice or medical care. They taught the arts of weaving and house building and carving to their kids. The food was in the river and the trees.

• • • • •

We gave them their first price for what we bought. That would be the village's currency income for the day, maybe the week. It took a lot of masks for a village to save up for something useful it could buy with currency, like an outboard motor.

• • • • •

"Where on earth are we?!"

"Mindimbit, isn't it?" Mirja thought, and it was true. We'd dropped anchor after dark just off the village of Mindimbit Number Two, which was supplied only by the river, no roads. Cooking fires were the only light along shore.

Now, everywhere is more plausible when you're there. It's out of the myth, apart from the hyperbole and in your face. We thought the same visiting the house of the Kumari, the living goddess in Kathmandu: THESE people are our fellow humans and THEY believe it....

Still, the Sepik River was hard to believe. At twilight we'd sit cross legged out front with Benny, the pilot. As gloom chased away the day, and the insects and creatures of the night emerged from the forests, the sky darkened but no light came up along the riverbank.

Furtive movement along the shoreline. One figure in white. A village passed starboard, in shapes more than seen. Finally, after the last light, each night became a monochrome blanket of inky sapphire.

Bugs collected around the windows by the millions. The deck would be thick as black snowfall with them in the morning.

•••••

Destination Angriman village, river glassy smooth. Before nine in the morning we crawled back onto the landing craft. As soon as they were off the big boat, the boys who came with us to the villages would break out the betel nut. They'd go full-animated as soon as they left the Sepik Spirit.

The people of Angriman were known up and down as the best crocodile hunters on the river. They raised them for their skin. When it was maybe four years old, a medium sized croc, fourteen inches around, might bring 200 kina from the Japanese agent who sailed in every three or four months.

The biggest would bring 300. Fifteen or 20 three-footers lay about in a wooden stockade.

Angriman produced watermelon, Malay apple trees, yams, mulberry bushes and a surplus of smoked fish. Mulberries were medicinal. You heated and inhaled them to treat a cold.

Leathery women smoked the fish on wire racks hung under the foundations of the houses. They'd stay edible that way for months.

•••••

The crocodile pen at Angriman.

Each Sepik village selected a councilman and the Sepik Council met every other month or so, sometimes at Karawari, sometimes at Timbunke. Collectively they elected a national representative to send to Port Moresby.

Peter Mai, the Angriman councilman, was a kind and generous fellow. We gave him a postcard of Atlanta with our address on the back and all his constituents and family promised to write. Four teenaged girls sang The Wonder of It All from a Seven Day Adventist hymnal, and then we stood in a receiving line as the villagers came to shake our hands.

The Seventh Day Adventists got here first. Just sailed right up the Sepik winning converts. Now they were losing ground to the Catholics because they'd tried to banish all the traditional beliefs. They wouldn't allow traditional dress.

With more fruit and vegetables than it needed, crocodiles for sale for currency and fish in exportable quantity, Angriman prospered. But Angriman wasn't served by a road and, unfortunately for Angriman, now it was no longer on the river.

The Sepik changed course some years back leaving Angriman, literally, a backwater, off the main channel. Still, fish and the crocodile trade had yielded wealth - Evinrude outboard motors attached to longboats.

Putting out and away from Angriman, the villagers waved and a Helmeted Friarbird called a "kowee ko keeyo" farewell. Back in the main channel a smiling family paddled by. An orange and white possum skittered up a tree. On the far bank a man chopped trees and rolled logs onto his longboat. A fish hawk flew close with a fish in his bill. A naked baby girl on the shore waved and yelled, "Ta ta!"

•••••

Upstream, anchored offshore from the village of Mindimbit (Number One, this time) for the night, we peered again into solitary blackness. Some of the villagers owned kerosene lamps, but kerosene wasn't something to be used lightly.

In the new day, Mindimbit was positively mercenary. One man had bought an immature cassowary, a blue-necked flightless, four-foot bird named Betty from Karawari. He charged a kina a camera for pictures. Prices were higher for artifacts and with the Sepik Spirit a sometimes visitor, Mindimbit was relatively grizzled at the curious westerner game.

Three Evinrudes and a Yamaha outboard were stashed in an open thatch shed. That said wealth.

A building of two-by-fours and four-by-fours stood framed but unfinished.

"They run out of money." Lawrence shook his head. Proper wood takes money. It's just not as practical as traditional houses lashed together with palms. With that kind of wood there was too much to buy. Like nails.

•••••

31

A man named Wesley invited us into his house. Up the stairs, (watch your head!) three women cooked lunch and minded the kids, all on the floor. A passing shower danced on the thatch overhead.

Ms. Julie smoked a split-open fish on a little round metal stove. Grandma minded a little boy and several pots and plates of greens. Wesley's wife made sago pancakes.

In the west it's bread. It's rice in Asia. In Papua New Guinea the basic food springs from the sago palm.

Sometimes the men fought over which Sago Palm to cut down. Finally they'd drag it to the village. It was skinned of its bark and chopped into hunks, then smaller hunks, then pummeled and pulverized to pulp, then sluiced through banana leaves into a paste and dried to a powder.

Between toothy smiles, Wesley's wife scooped the powder into a clay pot. A fire crackled underneath. With her cup she pressed it into pancakes. She'd lift each foot-long oval pancake off the oven and fold it in half. When it cooled we all tore edges off and popped them in our mouths. Captain Graeme said his wife added powdered coconut for a little flavor.

•••••

The next afternoon aboard the old landing craft, we caught up to the Sepik Spirit, which was waiting for us, tied to a tree near the Blackwater Lakes. The sun would set in half an hour. The river had smoothed for sunset.

Once we were aboard, Benny steered through swamp, short grass and expansive views. The banks rolled back to reveal mountains under white clouds. They say the Blackwater Lakes are black because of tannic acid that floats up from decaying plants.

We'd come from Mameri up on the north bank of the Sepik. It had a store where we bought matches and tobacco for the crew and curry for Lawrence.

Along the Sepik River.

There was a Sydney Morning Herald in the store dated March 28th. It was September. But this newspaper wasn't for reading. It was cigarette rolling paper. Three sheets sold for fifteen toea.

They offered a chew of betel nut. Amused men watched us split 'em open and pop the nuts into our mouths. You chew. That generates saliva, and you spit the juice through your teeth while keeping the meat.

The juice is white. You dip a couple-inch piece of mustard stalk into "lime," pounded from mussel shell, and chomp it. It turns the juice bright red. Chew, spit, chew. It's a little bitter and it gets your heart moving a bit, a little blood rushes to your head, everything's a notch more intense, and then it fades.

•••••

After it was full dark Mirja and Lawrence and I sat on rattan and cushions in the center of the Sepik Spirit. Canoes glided silently alongside, and their curious inhabitants, mostly adolescent boys, held their faces to the windows and peered inside. It was just the least bit disconcerting.

33

Lawrence had a story to tell.

"Now I will tell you about the way our elders taught us the secrets of the spirits."

First the disclaimer: "I was fourteen. I was working since I was twelve, with westerners. I ate western food. I did not believe there were spirits."

Still, at fourteen, there was room for doubt.

"It was frightening. We would start at six p.m. and they kept us awake until six in the morning. This went on for days.

"They built a wall in front of the spirit house with a door too small to walk through. One night they lit the palm fronds over the door into a fire and told us to run as fast as we could and squeeze through that little door, and not to get burned by the falling ashes.

"My grandfather was the leader of the village so I had to go first. Five boys were behind me. I was scared but I ran fast as I could go and I squeezed through that door and up the steps into the spirit house."

Squeezing through a door too small, Lawrence explained, symbolized the return to the mother's womb, because you must reunite with your mother's spirit as a rite of passage before your father can teach you all the spiritual secrets.

Mirja and I were a rapt audience.

"When we got inside the spirit house we got bad news. The men from the village were there and they were whipping us with canes to show us the power of each spirit. Ohhh, and it hurt!" Lawrence grimaced and held his forehead.

He pulled his legs up on the sofa and grew more animated.

"And now it was late, about five in the morning. They gave each boy a betel nut. My grandfather told me the one he gave me was a special one. They told us to chew them, it would be good for us. We spit out the juice and kept the meat inside our mouths.

"They gave us pieces of ginger and told us to chew them. They played drums and these flutes at the same time. I felt like maybe I had a gin and tonic!

"I was dizzy and then I started seeing skeletons dancing and then I had these incredible dreams. And I believe in Jesus and Mary but since that night I have also known that spirits are real, too."

•••••

Here is how the spirits communicate with Lawrence: "One night I heard someone say, 'Lawrence, get up and move your pillow.' He meant for me to put my head where my feet were and turn around.

"I woke up my wife and asked her if she said something and she said no. So I went back to sleep. I woke up again when I heard someone say, 'Lawrence, you missed your chance.'

"Another time I dreamed so clearly exactly what footsteps I should take. I would find a certain leaf and just underneath this certain shaped ginger. I walked to that spot and I looked under the leaf. And there it was just like in my dream."

•••••

The final part of gaining knowledge of the spirits is the skin cutting. You must ceremonially remove your mother's blood and give it back to her family, ending the power of her influence.

"We believe the father gives us the knowledge but the blood comes from the mother and so it must return to her. So my mother's brother came from another village.

"The night of the skin cutting we stayed up all night. When it was very late the men made us go into the water and stay for one hour so our skin would get soft. Ohhh, it was so cold!

Lawrence massaged his temples.

"When it was time I laid down on top of my mother's brother. So the blood would fall on him. And they cut me."

With a flourish he raised his right sleeve to show the results.

"Sometimes they cut your back but I asked they only cut my arms because I had to go back to work."

He had to have time to heal.

But he didn't heal. He was infected.

"I asked for medicine but my grandfather refused. He asked me, 'What have you done wrong?' I said nothing, nothing over and over but he kept asking me until finally I admitted I had stayed with my girlfriend the night before.

"Before they would use sharp bamboo leaves but now they use razors. I asked my grandfather if the razor was old but he said no it was bought new for this purpose. My infection was punishment for this bad act."

Lawrence really, reverently believed it.

"After some days I washed it with salt and warm water and finally it was okay."

•••••

Lawrence thought the missionaries were wrong to exclude the possibility that other religious beliefs may be true. And in the forests and on the rivers of Papua New Guinea, where when darkness falls it plummets, spirits lurked more than down any American highway.

His grandfather, who Lawrence called, "A famous headhunter," told him at the end of his weeks of spiritual training (spiritual training can take six months, but Lawrence had to get back to his job) that he would have unbelievable opportunities in the future.

One of the people he had led on a cruise like this recently offered him a trip to the U.S., and to Lawrence, that was proof positive it was so.

•••••

4 BHUTAN

Only about thirty of us were flying to Bhutan, so the back of the plane held cargo: a couple of computers strapped to the seats, a boom box, a crock pot, several unmarked boxes, a quilt. And in the back seat a flight attendant drank in sleep - I mean, she snored. She, Mirja and one more were the only women.

The river Brahmaputra wound out toward the Ganges near Dhaka. Sunlight glinted and skipped across tens of thousands of acres of flooded rice paddies, miles and miles north of the Bay of Bengal. Sometimes the clouds lifted over northern Burma and Bangladesh.

Four hundred miles north of Rangoon a bend in the river ate half a town. It was July 4th. Americans celebrated independence while South Asia grappled with the monsoon.

When time came to drop through the clouds into Bhutan, the pilot announced, "We will maneuver the aircraft in the valley. This is a little different from large commercial aircraft. It is standard procedure. You will see the houses and trees a little closer than you are used to. The scenery is beautiful. Please enjoy the ride."

He just picked a hole in the clouds and dove through. He did a 180 into the Paro valley. The automatic sensors called out, "too low," and for the record he kept repeating, "acknowledge, override," into the cockpit recorder.

This was George, bluff, barrel-chested, a real dude with a wide gray mustache, and one of just fourteen people ever to fly for Royal Bhutan Airlines, aka Druk Air. We said we'd buy him a beer if we saw him in town and he told us he'd drink it.

The only airport in Bhutan is in Paro, an old west one-horse town spread three hundred feet, and no more, across the valley floor, hardly movin' in the midday sun. Uniformed

Indian soldiers lolled about drinking "Thums Up" brand cola.

•••••

Phruba and Jigme, our guide and driver for the week, gathered us up for the trip to Thimpu, the capital and main city. Irrigated rice grew just about before your eyes, and every river was a tumult.

We crept and powered around corners (all week) in a Toyota Yokohama van. Jigme and Phruba both wore traditional skirt-like wraps called ghos, a lot like Burmese longyis (chapter six). Phruba's legs stuck out below the knee. All week long he sat in the passenger seat, the picture of Buddhism, calm, legs hairy and hands clasped.

Tall and 28, he used to play basketball with the young King.

"We would stay outside and pick teams," Phruba told us. "When he was in a good mood the King would invite us in to play. When he was in a bad mood he would play with his bodyguards. He is very good at the three point shot."

Being taller than the King sets up a sensitive question: Does one shoot over the King's head? Yes. The King's bodyguards are some of the biggest men in the country, Phruba said, so he reckoned the King was used to it.

•••••

"Phruba, is the King married?" Mirja wanted to know.

"Yes, he has four Queens" Phruba replied, and seeing an eyebrow cock, he tried to put that right by adding what must have seemed the obvious: "But they are all sisters."

With only one newspaper in the country, Kuensel, a weekly that comes out on Saturdays, how does Phruba keep up with the world? His answer was simple, disarming and direct.

Phruba's eyes twinkled. He laughed, "We don't. We don't read much."

The national dish is called Ema Datse, literally chillies and cheese (It's those long not-too-hot green chillies we call "finger hot" in a bowl of melted cheese, eaten with a spoon). Discovering our common love of chillies, Phruba's face fairly radiated. "Whenever people travel outside of Bhutan they carry chilli powder. To Bangladesh, India, Bengal - anywhere!"

Whether they travel to India or Bengal, Bhutanese bring back a lot of India. Everything not Bhutanese was Indian: The uniformed soldiers in Paro, those horrid polluting Tata buses and the big cement-truck look-alikes used for general transport, all of them spewing the same ghastly black smoke that's already spoiled, say, the Kathmandu valley.

There's Mysore Rose Brand soap. Dansberg beers. Indian videos - there were posters for Suraj! and Insaaf - The Final Justice! and Border! All with exclamation marks!

And rupees.

The Ngultrum (Bhutanese money) is pegged to the Indian Rupee and you can spend either of them. Bhutanese share Indian punctiliousness and an inclination to paperwork. Pads of every kind of paperwork are done in triplicate with carbons - even restaurant orders.

•••••

They're trying to keep Bhutan pure. I think intellectually everybody knows it's a losing long-term proposition, but good for them just the same. In a lot of ways it's working.

Most men wear traditional ghos. Guys walk together with an arm around their buddy's waist. You get benevolent, open stares. So few people have stuck Nikons in their faces that they still smile back.

•••••

An hour and a half from the airport the Toyota rattled up the driveway of the Indigenous Art School. Trying to keep traditional ways alive, the government brings children who show talent here from all over the country to learn to create religious thangkas, or paintings, and to learn carving and sculpting.

Here they all sat, at wooden benches, windows wide open - no electricity in the building - working in natural light. We stopped methodically at year 1 year 2 year 3 year 4 year 5 and so on up to eight. Smiling boys in robes at dusty wood benches. A fairy tale.

•••••

There was a football match that afternoon. You could hear the stadium cheer from every corner of Thimpu. Phruba boasted (or did he rue?) that it was up to 27,000 or 28,000 now, Thimpu was. No stoplights yet, but there were two traffic cops. A sign on the road between them advised, "Dumping Strongly Prohibited."

I treaded mud down toward the sound of the crowd, down by the river, the Wang Chhu, admission fee 5 Ngultrums (14 cents), and sat with four monks from India, each contributing to the betel-juice-stain emergency in Thimpu.

•••••

A delicate, clean rain began as the football match let out, and for a little while the streets of Thimpu (only a few streets), teemed. At the Phuntsho Meat Shop a man stood under naked light bulbs on a table high above the buying public wielding an ancient scale, weighing skinned chickens and fish.

I walked into the bar at the Hotel Taksang, directly opposite Pelwang's Mini Mart and below the billboard explaining the "Sewerage Construction Project – for better health." They already knew I lived in room 325 and they told me my wife was asleep upstairs. I was the only one there and they made french fries to go with my beer. In this bar one beer cost 54 ngultrums and two cost 104.

Stray dogs (I think about eight billion) gave a free, full-throated concert most nights. Strays are the bane of Bhutan, just like in Kathmandu and Rangoon and Tahiti.

Being Buddhist, the Bhutanese have a little problem. They can't kill the strays, can't even spay them. That would be taking a life. But they can appoint Indian Hindus as dog catchers, and have them kill dogs on the pretense of rabies or rash.

The Phuntsho Meat Shop, Thimpu.

Neither tumultuous, chaotic nor edgy, the polite weekend market sold no disgusting pounded meats or goats' heads or bowls full of crawling bugs. Everybody wore their traditional clothes and chewed betel.

One guy sat sorting fat green chillies. He'd pause and turn, spit betel juice in his right hand, shake it behind him, and dig right back into the chillies.

A short drive from the river, the only golf course in Bhutan doubled as the front yard for the Supreme Court. Across the road at the Indigenous Medicine Hospital (established in 1978 by the World Health Organization) the manager tried to integrate the traditional and the modern. If patients didn't get well via one regimen, he tried the other.

They grew all their own herbal remedies in a garden out back. There were machines from Austria to package them. Three rooms were labeled like this: Powder Section No Admittance, Pills Section No Admittance, Tablet Section No Admittance.

A prayer wheel clanged because they always turned it, the patients sitting in the courtyard, which doubled as the waiting room.

Twenty or thirty people mashed bark into pulp at the oxymoronic "Jungshi Handmade Paper Factory." They wet it, dried it, rolled it, spread it, and eventually produced coarse papers, some embedded with leaves or rose petals.

Down at Plum's Café, you could read a three day old Times of India. It was the most up-to-date news in Bhutan. You could sit on a toilet named Hindware. Ex-pats and their kids took up too much space and fretted in the corner. Probably the calmest posting in the world, and still they fretted.

•••••

Up the hill, past the embassies of Bangladesh and Denmark, the Little Dragon Montessori School, the Druk Incense Unit (manufacturing and exporting) and the Motithang Fire Out Post, was a sanctuary for the mysterious cross between the sheep and yak - not the shack - the Golden Takin, preserved for its own safety in this place, behind a fence, some time ago when animal diseases spread across Bhutan.

Down on the valley floor, prayer flags flapped from a government telecommunications tower. Paddies ran right up to the Royal Palace.

The Royal Compound, Thimpu

Phruba declared that no subject has seen inside the palace. Mirja and I chewed on this for a while. Whattaya think's inside? Jacuzzis?

You think they live like what, kings?!

•••••

For goodness sake, don't ever quote me on Buddhism, and Phruba suggested we not quote him on spelling the names of the Bodhisattvas either, but at a nunnery and a monastery, here is what I understood: Girls can become nuns by the same rules that boys become monks - same rules for either sex.

The Dub Thub nunnery on the hill honored a fifteenth century Bodhisattva named Tonton Gyalpu.

"He built all the chain bridges in Bhutan," Phruba explained, "But only one still exists, in eastern Bhutan."

A cloth draped over one whole wall was "to protect dust and to keep out the breath."

45

On the right of the altar, Phruba told us, pointing left, was a painting of a sixteenth century reincarnation of Tonton Gyalpu. Just below it was a 1994 calendar with a picture of the current reincarnation, now 17, who had left a month ago for a tour of the United States. On the left, he said, gesturing right, more pictures of the Bodhisattva.

Gods and men can be thirsty. Bowls of water, brought in at sunrise and out at dark, lined the altar as offerings. A bow to ancient Bon beliefs sat right atop the altar - peacock feathers and tree branches.

There were ceremonies four times a day at the Dub Thub nunnery, and flies twenty four hours. If you wanted your own ceremony, for good luck in a new job, for example, or in ill health, it could be arranged with just an offering of money and tea for the monks and nuns. Outside, nun's wraps draped over the railing.

•••••

Bumping along the way to the next monastery, Mirja drew from her standard repertoire.

"Do you have snakes?"

"Oh yes!"

"Poisonous ones?"

"Yes, cobras!"

•••••

The Queens' personal monastery, on a bluff over Thimpu town, honors a Bodhisattva named Avaloktsherwa, the "Buddha of Compassion" who you'll see with nine heads, or eleven, or one thousand. He vowed to eliminate all human suffering and when he realized the enormity of his vow, Phruba said, "his head was exploded."

Somehow, that's why you see him today with nine heads, or eleven, or one thousand.

"You come here (to the Queens' monastery) to get names," Phruba explained. The monks name babies in a formula according to the year.

As we walked in, a young woman threw dice onto a plate held by a monk. Phruba observed for a while.

"That girl has exams starting tomorrow. She is seeing if she will do well."

As far as monasteries go, Phruba confided, "I trust this one more."

•••••

Back at the hotel, a savage fight broke out at the sewer construction site. A woman or two screamed, shouted at their men and slammed some car doors. The Buddhists watched in awe, and they shook their heads at the wrath and passion of the Indians.

Still, they needed them.

"Bhutanese people are great at many things," Phruba declared, "But not with concrete."

So the workers were Indian or Nepali, but that was a problem, because everybody in Bhutan knew that once they came, they would never leave. Free education and medicine made for better living. They would put on ghos or kiras, the women's traditional dress, and it would be hard to tell if they were Bhutanese or not.

There is a derogatory term for these people, ngolops. All the district borders within Bhutan had checkpoints to try to prevent ngolops' movement within the country. The weekly newspaper Kuensel always reported on parliamentary debates about ngolops.

I asked Phruba the pronunciation of "ngolop." He pronounced it for me ("no - lop"), thought for a moment more, then told me, "It is better not to say that word."

•••••

Indian music woke us, really loud and really early. I trudged downstairs to the breakfast room and sat at the window, staring sullenly at a man inside his apartment across the street because I thought he was the source of the music. He glared back at me.

I asked for orange juice and it came back grapefruit.

Phruba came in with a warning: We're going east, and outside of western Bhutan you'll have to be ready for toilets with buckets and maybe you can ask for a bucket to wash with.

•••••

Dzongs are fortresses, one for every main town. Our destination was the biggest one in Bhutan, the Trongsa dzong. We climbed a pass toward Lobesa, a shimmering green little place where they've grown apples, oranges and brown jacket cardamom, exports to Bangladesh, for eight or nine years.

An immigration checkpoint to find ngolops stood at Angtso. We pulled up behind an impossibly full van and stopped to wait beside Gakey Restaurant Bar and Grocery House #3.

A prayer wheel in a little concrete hut at the edge of the road turned by water power. This was terribly auspicious for the guy who built it because the more you turn a prayer wheel the better. He was set for life, or at least the life of the stream. People have even used tap water to turn prayer wheels, Phruba allowed, but that's problematic now that they've started charging for water.

The road climbed to just over ten thousand feet, where the Dochula Pass was wholly swallowed in mist, an achromatic, ghostly place. The road, intermittently paved, was ever only eight or ten feet wide, and the ubiquitous honking before heading into hairpin turns was little beyond talismanic. Surely somebody above and 270 degrees around a switchback wouldn't hear.

Wattle fence, to check landslides, ringed the road. Blue plastic canvas served as tents for road laborers, 130 ngultrum-a-day sentinels of misery, all wet all day every day way up here in the clouds.

Even on the most obscure patch of earth (and they had plenty of them), there'd be a painted background on the overhanging rocks, say a red rectangle overlaid with yellow Bhutanese script spelling out the six syllable mantra Om Mani Padme Hum, which for Buddhists purifies the six realms of existence, the worlds of God, God and human, human, animals, hungry ghosts and hell.

At the village of Thinlegang, workers bent nearly double in the paddies. Jigme pulled to the side of the road, jumped out, fired up a cigarette and tried tuning his shortwave radio.

"What's on?" I asked.

"Nothing sir," he exclaimed brightly. I could tell that, but I meant what was he trying to find.

"It's Sunday. Our Bhutan national broadcast. I think it's too early. Maybe at ten."

After the road junction to the former capital of Punakha, we came alongside the massive Punak Chhu (chhu means river) as it lumbered through bottomland, bound for the Brahmaputra, Ganges and ultimately the Bay of Bengal. Beyond the Punak Chhu checkpoint we climbed, retracing the opposite side of the river up into the garrison town of Wangdi Phodrang.

Wangdi is Bhutan's main military town. Indian troops train the Bhutanese army. A sign reads, "Join the Army and Serve the Nation."

Jigme stopped to gas up the Yokohama and pick up box lunches. He reckoned it would be four and a half hours until the next shop, so we bought litres of Gold Star Water, a product of Eastern Traders, 44 Exra Street, Calcutta. Mirja thought it sounded like motor oil.

Wangdi was lined with ramshackle Indian-style trading stalls that Barbara Crossette (in her book *So Close to Heaven*) kindly observed, "defy all attempts to define them as quaint."

There are two versions of how Wangdi (or Wangdue, as you'll also see it) Phodrang got its name: One is that a 17th century leader, or Shabdrung, saw a boy building a castle with sticks and asked his name. The boy said Wangdi and the town was named for him, Wangdi's castle. Or if you prefer, it's because the dzong was built in a place where you can see all four directions, another meaning of Wangdi.

We had the requisite car trouble leaving town, but it was nothing a few whacks on the battery cables with a tire tool couldn't fix, and we were off for Trongsa.

Mountain goats mingled with the cattle that roamed the roads. Somewhere we stopped and ate lunch on a hill. The inevitable pack of kids found us, marked out its distance, and stood and stared. They wouldn't come closer and they wouldn't talk until we left, when they hit us with a torrent of "Ok bye bye see you tomorrow!"

•••••

Time, language and numbers all had a random way in Bhutan. Ask Jigme and Phruba how long today's drive would last and you'd hear ten and eight hours (It took a little more than seven). Along one stretch of particularly hellish road Mirja thought Jigme was in danger of dozing off, so she peppered the boys with random questions. One was how many employees their company had.

Phruba: "We have fifteen. Twelve guides, nine drivers, and we have trekking staff, office staff...."

In transliteration, "r's" in particular come and go. Our destination was Tongsa on the map, Trongsa on the road signs. The signs gave a running count of the distance to Trashigang. The maps read Tashigang.

•••••

Way up in the fog, we rolled to a stop in front of six mildewed men with sledgehammers. They faced huge rocks in the middle of the road. They'd just cleared a tiny gap, and we picked our way through. Two huge Indian transport trucks full of logs came barreling around us down toward the slide. If they got through I'd have to see it to believe it.

Phruba piled us out onto the side of the road above a village called Rukubji to explain how a crazy spirit had visited there and had not been treated well. He cast a spell and that's why the fine people of Rukubji cannot to this day grow rice. They grow wheat, and potatoes.

Stupa outside Rukubji.

While Phruba was storytelling, Jigme found the Bhutan Broadcasting Service and a music program. "Bhutan disco," he smiled. (Jigme preferred his nickname, roughly pronounced "Pudt-so." It meant, same as it sounds in English, roughly "short and round.")

Finally, we all got to unwind and stretch at the Sherubling Tourist Lodge, nestled on a hill just below the Trongsa high school. They brought us tea and Ritz crackers. We'd just taken most of the day to bounce 194 hard-fought kilometers.

The dzong itself is off limits to tourists, for it's a very important place both religiously and politically. But there is a watchtower way up above that you can visit. It holds a monastery for healing the sick.

Up the muddy path, then up the nearly vertical monastic ladder steps, seven monks were just preparing to conduct a ceremony for the living, the dying and the dead, complete with horns, bells and drum.

They said we could stay and served yak butter tea. They chanted endless passages from memory, the natural afternoon light flooding through the windows, and made music until far after we had climbed back down the hill. Really fabulous.

Down in the town now. Only one real street. More ads for Indian videos "Auzaar" and "Ziddi." A discarded box that once held "Aroma School Shoes."

Phruba vaguely explained a game monks play with four balls and a stick. He pointed out cedar trees down by the dzong. cedars are the national tree of Bhutan. There was a time when they exported them to Tibet in exchange for religious teachers.

Four young women wove yak wool into colored patterns on ancient wooden looms at Tashi Tsering General Shop and Bar. I scared them with my camera flash and they giggled. An old man tried to get us to buy from his shop. He was another example of why the book Dental Arts in Bhutan would be more of a pamphlet.

Phruba told us as far as he knew we were the first westerners here since the sixth of June when he brought some French folks up. That would have been a little more than a month.

•••••

When the day came to an end, we sat in the dusk on log benches, barefoot in the wet grass. While we watched, mist first enveloped the river valley, then veiled the town, the dzong, and finally crept right up to where we sat.

Nema, the slightly sodden hotelier, served dinner. Mirja thought her Golden Eagle Lager (of India) tasted "like our room smells." She had a good point. You could smell the past in all the rooms in Trongsa.

Probably unwisely, I dipped into a half liter bottle of Jaching Brandy, produce of Bhutan, "Blended and Bottled by Army Welfare Project Gaylegphug Distillery." We ordered our hot water for 7:30 a.m., left our empty bucket outside the door and fell asleep in the rain.

•••••

The Trongsa dzong dated back centuries but it had been rebuilt lots of times, after fires from overturned butter lamps and a huge earthquake that leveled just about all the dzongs. Nowadays the Trongsa dzong had electricity and plumbing (The dzong in Paro, where the airport is, was just now getting power).

It was the heart of the nation. The first King of Bhutan was the governor of Trongsa, ruling from the dzong, when he overthrew the last Shabdrung to unify the Kingdom. The third King, the reigning King's father, was born here. All kings did a stint here as governor before accession to the throne.

Although Bhutan has only been ruled as a Kingdom for a hundred years, it has had a sense of nation since the eighth century. In Papua New Guinea, nobody knew anyone in the next valley. PNG'ers were animists. Bhutanese had the bond of Buddha.

•••••

First light showed it had rained all night. Water dripped through the leaves, peaceful and delightful, but I worried that now maybe the road back was washed out.

A man in Punakha, the former capital, told me that when he was a tour guide in Trongsa in 1991, the most landslides ever happened. They finally airlifted the tourists out but it was a week before they reopened the road.

Maybe we'd stay in Trongsa, with our bucket, for some time.

"We have no helicopters in Bhutan," Phruba declared preemptively. Just in case.

•••••

We made it out, and all the way to Punakha. It rained all day.

We didn't pass another vehicle for more than two hours. People used the road to spread reeds and weave mats.

The rains energized the hills. Waterfalls appeared by the hundreds, thousands, and even more in secret little places across the valley, here now, covered and gone in a minute, dropping hundreds of feet at a bound.

We only passed two trucks the whole morning, instead mostly confronting cattle and horses run by muddy boys. Sometimes white stripes marked the center of the road, with four feet on each side.

•••••

The Pele Pass crouched shrouded in simple, utter fog. We crept around to the previous day's slide. A new boulder the length of two men, waist high, lay across the road. Men from one of the blue canvas huts were beating on it. This was gonna take a while.

Jigme entered negotiations. Four or five sticks of dynamite materialized and were slapped on the rock and held in place by mud. Phruba, Mirja and I scurried back. Jigme rolled the van back around the corner to a place with no rocks above it. We waited.

Dynamiting the road at the Pele Pass.

The blast rocked down and back up the valley and rocked us in our chests. It shook smaller pines out of the ground and sent them skittering down the hill in a hundred places. It cracked the rock. We crept around the corner and just then, shouts. Five men scattered in a flutter of ghos as clots of earth and rocks tumbled straight toward them, dragging a young pine behind.

Gingerly, they returned. In subdued triumph they laid the tree, cautiously, across the rocks they'd piled on the lip of the canyon.

Forty five minutes later a call went out. They'd pried and stacked enough of the boulder away that we could just squeeze though, barely.

•••••

Punakha made a dismal capital city, and Phruba said the third King knew it, so in 1955 he moved the capital to the broad Thimpu valley, giving it room to grow. Phruba rued that his own grandfather, who had land in both places, built the sprawling family house in Punakha, the capital, and only a small hut in Thimpu.

The hotel in Punakha had telephones, though. They didn't connect to anywhere but the front desk and Phruba failed to raise the outside world via the radiophone behind the reception desk, but that was okay, the management used the hell out of 'em.

"What time would you like dinner?" One call.

"What would you like for dinner?" Two.

Three: "Would you like your papads baked or fried?"

The morning calls started at 7:10 (We ordered 8:30 breakfast) but I don't know what they wanted because we ignored them.

The Hotel Zangdho Pelri was owned by the parents of the four Queens.

Perhaps a word on why there are four Queens: In Bhutan, you marry the eldest sister in a family and her sisters also become your wives. Property is handed down to the females, not the males. Marrying all the females in the family is a way for the family's wealth not to be diluted.

"It stays in," says Phruba. "It doesn't matter how many sisters, three, four, five - only one husband comes in."

It isn't always done everywhere anymore, he says, but absolutely still is in the more remote spots.

Mirja asked, "Do the Queens do charity work or anything?"

Phruba looked right back and told her, "No, they just live." Sometimes they'll open a business or a hospital if they're asked, he allowed.

•••••

We planned a morning walk to the fifteenth century monastery called Chimmi between Punakha and Lobesa, high on a hill. Then we'd walk back through villages, ending at the Punakha dzong.

But an insistent rain gave us time instead to ponder things like the government policy of allowing 4000 visitors a year, which equals 77 a week nationwide. Based on how many vacationers we'd seen - three besides us - they could go wild and let in a hundred next week.

•••••

Punakha dzong sat at the confluence of the larger Mo (mother) and Pho (father) rivers. A suspension footbridge crossed the Mo, which coursed full-speed not two meters below your feet. It was at its highest just now, during the monsoon.

Phruba grinned. "This river also flows to the Brahmaputra. It is our water that floods Bangladesh."

One end of the Punakha dzong has been under semi-permanent construction. In 1994, six or eight prisoners on the construction detail died when their jail flooded. Phruba told us straight up, it was because they were trapped in chains.

Barbara Crossette writes that Bhutan was astonished to learn everybody didn't chain their prisoners and when they found out, they immediately quit, embarrassed.

At the confluence of the Mo and Pho Rivers.

Until 1955 Punakha dzong ruled the country. Inside the center tower are no less than 28 temples and the biggest thangka in Bhutan, extending nearly all the way up the inside of the tower. It celebrates the eight original clans united into a nation.

Here Phruba got talking fast about a special ceremony with eight warriors, one from each of the clans, and how today they still have three days of absolute power. "They can even kill someone," he told us.

Guru Rinpoche, who is said to have brought Buddhism to Bhutan, predicted by name that Shabdrung Namgyal, the unifier and first of eight Shabdrungs preceding the royal family, would build a temple at the spot he called Elephant Hill (it does slope like the head and back of an elephant). And Shabdrung Namgyal did have this dzong built.

But in 1651 when he died, the elders were afraid that if the people learned of the great unifier's death the country might come apart. So they faked his continued health. Since that moment of his death, in 1651, the people haven't been able to go into the special temple where his body (we guess) still rests. There are those who still invest supernatural powers in

Shabdrung Namgyal and believe he still lives, just inside this chamber.

•••••

A dzong mixes church and state. It's a monks' residence and the seat of state government. There's a tower containing the temples with a building built around it, incorporating a courtyard inside. One side of the tower is the administration for the state and the other is for the monks. The courtyards are for observances and festivals.

The governor's office is inside, the first right. A stupa stands straight ahead in the courtyard. Here's the vagueness of time in the Kingdom of the Thunder Dragon: Phruba explained that "this chorten (stupa) was built in 1982 by the Queen Mother as a memorial to a very holy man who died in 1984."

The guards, one of them with a fifteen-inch dagger on the end of his rifle, were just boys. I asked Phruba what kind of guards they were. "Royal Bhutan Police," he exclaimed. "Most of them are over fifteen years old."

•••••

In Bhutan, mysticism remains the coin of the realm.

For centuries Bhutanese women unable to conceive have come to spend the night alone inside the Chummi monastery. Somehow, it's also famous in Japan. Not long ago a Japanese woman came here, went home, had a child and named it Chummi.

A boy in the Bumthang valley is known to be a reincarnation of his neighbor's bull. He goes next door and gets down on all fours and he knew the name of the bull without being told.

The 68th head Abbot, or the Je Rhenpo, died three months ago in meditation. You don't cremate someone who dies in meditation because he may not be finished.

Although, Phruba swears, "His jaws sag and he's lost some body weight," he's still posed kneeling in the same spot right now, today, in Timphu. When he falls over they'll cremate him.

•••••

Still it poured in Punakha. Jigme found out the National Archery Finals were this afternoon in Thimpu.

"What time?" I asked. Phruba looked puzzled. I guessed it'd be on when we arrived, and it was.

On the way we stopped to see a dart match in the mud, the local team in a tight match with the bad guys in the village of Thinlet Gang.

The archery finals pitted Druk Air versus the Agriculture Ministry, these two teams winnowed from the original eight. Rain couldn't dampen spirits, but not a gho on the grounds smelled fresh.

Spectators at the archery finals.

A pickup team played football against the police. The whole town was there. It was a holiday. The sun even broke through. The afternoon turned beautiful as we set off for Paro. But I must say, I've NEVER seen so much traffic in Bhutan.

Phruba rued progress.

•••••

Setting out on foot from a stream on the Paro valley floor, Mirja, Phruba and I hiked up to an elevation of 3000 meters, at first along stream beds and through pine forests, then out across the sturdy red soil. The sun beat down and the air was perfectly still.

Phruba told us to stick to the main path - the shortcuts are too steep - and right away he fell back, only to appear ahead of us via a shortcut. Old guide trick.

We were alone as always, passing only two women and a boy resting by a prayer wheel. They were walking on to the Tiger's Nest monastery to stay the night.

The Tiger's Nest is just impossible, perched on a sheer hill. We gazed across a valley from a lookout point. I didn't think I could walk to it, let alone carry on my back enough materials to build it.

There was a little cafeteria at the lookout point, which was the terminus for all but pilgrims and monks. The cook rustled up a delicious vegetarian lunch, and we sat at a little terrace and demonstrated our cameras to the assorted few who lived up here in support of the cafeteria/gift shop/outpost.

Phruba told us that at Tiger's Nest, "Ceremony day after (He meant tomorrow) for weather making. It is big this year because this year we have two Junes." He paused. "Sometimes we have no August."

Excuse me?

He knew he had us and he warmed to the subject.

"Oh yes. Today is the ninth. Maybe sometimes we have two ninths and maybe no eleventh. This is decided by the monks and they always agree."

It's published in Kuensel every Saturday, so you have to check.

"This is why you cannot know when are the festivals."

•••••

We drove to the national museum, perched on a hilltop above the Paro dzong, (also called the Rinchen Pung dzong, or "fortress on a heap of jewels"). From 1651 it had served as a watchtower. Thunder cracked across the valley and rain pelted the roof of the museum's top floor, the stamp gallery.

Here were stamps commemorating: the 250th anniversary of the birth of George Washington, the Innsbruck 1976 Olympic Games, mushrooms (in 3-D), countless coronations, various non-aligned summits, the rose (scented), Apollo XVII (3-D), talking stamps (tiny phonograph records), international popular dogs, the 60th anniversary of the Boy Scouts, classic cars (3-D), insects (3-D), steelmaking, the Battle of Britain, and the Yeti.

Chains from a chain bridge (one of the eight of which only one remains) built by Saint Drupthob Thangtong Gyalpu (1385-1464) were on display. So was what they called an ancient water clock. It was a bowl into which 60 drops of water were placed. When they had evaporated, an hour had passed.

There were skulls or stuffed versions of indigenous animals, like the very endangered snow leopard, the barking deer, guar, alligator, wild yak and Tibetan gazelle.

In 1872 the future first King was imprisoned for six months by the eighth, and last Shabdrung, in the basement.

And there was this item, just so you know: "Self imbossed conch shell believed to be a tooth of Terton Pema Lingpa (1450-1521)."

•••••

Inside the Paro dzong, boy monks played in the courtyard, the bigger ones stealing the smaller ones' wraps, to hold out and wet in the rain where the gutters didn't work. An ancient hall smelled that way, open, wood floored, with the stink of dirty wet boys of questionable hygiene.

Phruba had changed from his hiking clothes to his gho to enter the dzong. He was explaining how the high threshold at entrances to dzongs everywhere was essentially to keep Tibetans out in times of war, since they wore lower skirts than Bhutanese men, making it slower for them to step over the thresholds when invading.

As he told us, Phruba unwrapped the sash all Bhutanese men wear around their ghos in monasteries as a sign of respect. Another use of the high threshold: He began, "When we have our dead people...." and right there the only cross moment among Bhutanese flared because a Royal Bhutan Police monastery guard accosted Phruba demanding he put his sash back on.

They talked all in Dzongka and we just left them to argue, walking away up the hill.

•••••

Settling up at the front desk at the Hotel Olthang, I was waiting for my less than one dollar change (more than they ever seemed to keep behind any counter. They were forever having to run next door or down the hall to make change. This particular time they didn't have Ng32 where Ng35 = $1).

The Indian guys beside me were in full rage, shouting "Give me that money please," and grabbing at a wad the night clerk held back wide-eyed. They demanded a quarter of five wake up call and thundered that if you don't call us we'll miss our flight.

They made it. Both planes in the Druk Air fleet were in Paro the next morning. Our buddy George the pilot was off for Kathmandu, while we left for Calcutta. There were no x-ray machines.

Leaving Bhutan requires a little airplane acrobatics. Just into the air you must lean left, around the hill at the end of the runway, then lean left down the valley, back and forth for five minutes until you clear the hills.

Druk Air served spring rolls and salad for breakfast - with a croissant.

• • • • •

5 THE TRANS-SIBERIAN RAILWAY

If you don't speak Russian and if you decode Cyrillic gingerly, one letter at a time, it's not completely effortless to come up with bottled water in Ekaterinburg, but it is possible, and I bought six litres.

The kiosk, alongside a tram stop, was just big enough to be a walk-in affair, not big enough for four, let alone our steamy tensome. The boys in front argued over what beer and candy to order one each of. I motioned for six bottles way up high on a shelf and all kinds of consternation rippled through the mottled impatience behind me.

In a few hours Mirja and I would be climbing aboard the Trans-Siberian railroad to Ulan Bataar, Mongolia. We'd be a week en route, so we needed all kinds of stuff.

As soon as I had all those bottles, though, I calculated we could get everything else at the train station. Six litres of water is heavy.

Today was Labor Day in the U.S. On the edge of Siberia, autumn held full sway. E-kat's denizens plodded by cold and damp in an insistent, heavy shower. A lot of the older folks wore long coats. All day the rain beset.

•••••

Every account of coming upon the Ural mountains speaks of disappointment, and for good reason. The dividing line between Europe and Asia is just hills, really, and Ekaterinburg nestles just beyond their eastern slopes.

The Atrium Palace Hotel Ekaterinburg looked so nice on the internet that we mused back home that it had to be either German or mafia owned. Well, it wasn't German. It was E-kat's only "5-star," with glass elevators and snuggly, fluffy Scandinavian bedding and BBC World on TV.

Still, it had its Russian characteristics: There was the hourly rate, Rule #2: "If you stay for less than six hours, you are charged for twelve hour accommodation." And Rule #7: "The guests who troubled a lot before can not be allowed to stay at the hotel." Hard to know if the guys in track suits grouped around the lobby drinking coffee were part of the problem or there to enforce the solution.

•••••

Mid-rises glowered down on ancient Siberian carved–wood houses. There wasn't much spring in E-kat's civic step. Down Ulitsa Malysheva, a second-tier comrade (maybe it was Malysheva himself) stood statuary guard near a canal. The flowers at his feet had long since conceded to summer weeds.

Old and dusty women tended the old and dusty local history museum. They turned the lights on and off as you moved through the rooms. The Communism section was closed.

During the revolution, in July 1918, The entire family of deposed Czar Nicholas was shot while holed up at the home of a merchant named Ipatiev here in Ekaterinburg - then called Sverdlovsk - and some days later the besieged Bolsheviks burned and buried the bodies outside town.

In 1977, local Sverdlovsk party boss Boris Yeltsin ordered the Ipatiev House destroyed. Fourteen years later Yeltsin, then in the Kremlin, financed exhumation of the bodies from the burial pit, and exactly eighty years after their murder, on July 17, 1998 the bones of Russia's last Czar were laid beside the bones of previous Czars in the crypt of the Peter and Paul Cathedral in St. Petersburg. In the museum, black and white pictures of Nicholas and Alexandra were pinned up alongside diagrams of skeletons.

In a dainty candle-lit Orthodox church-let, hardly big enough for the two women inside, Mirja and I bought a tiny cross and a few icons. With a glass, the women inspected the back of each, like kids examine trading cards, and they proclaimed one Nikolai and explained of another, "Blogodot Denyaba."

E-kat's youth did a kind of country swagger beneath a huge billboard for "Ural Westcom" Cellular – written in Latin, not Cyrillic. Every kid in town walked up and down the sidewalk drinking big brown half litre bottles of beer. Maybe it was because they could.

Muddy Ekaterinburg, east of the Urals.

If your baseline was vodka, pivo (beer) was positively a soft drink in comparison. None of these young people – old enough to aspire to fashion and to drink and flirt and smoke – none of them remembered the days of vodka and The State. They were all eight or twelve at the Soviet Union's demise.

The train station was white, granite and huge, a city block long and probably more, but it was hard to see why - they only used a tiny slice of it. There was just time to lug our stuff into the steamy waiting hall, and before you knew it, up rolled train number two, the Rossiya.

Here was a moment of some import. They told us our first class compartment was "very expensive," but we didn't care about that (it wasn't that expensive), we just wanted to find it very empty. And so it was.

The woman under whose iron will Trans-Siberian lore demanded we cower - the provodnitsa - while no nonsense, appeared kindly enough as she studied our tickets, nodded, and handed over the key to cabin nine, between cabin eight, with a baby, and the toilet.

Inside - impeccably clean. Mirrors on each wall made a not very big space bigger. All six lights worked – the overhead fluorescent, lights on the walls, and tiny reading lights over each bunk.

The window was structurally shut and it was warmer than it needed to be. Satiny print curtains covered the window but Mirja moved them above the door. That way we could have it open and see out, but people in the corridor couldn't see in. Brilliant.

A small writing/eating table. Bunks with bedding, the rough blankets in a Scottish tartan pattern.

Home sweet home on the Trans-Siberian.

A samovar sat at the provodnitsa's end of each car (ours with bits of drying, fresh-picked wild mushrooms arrayed across the top) to provide water for chai or coffee. I'd remembered every possible gadget, but I'd forgotten plates and towels. I stole a towel and paid good money for plates from the hotel, but there was a plate with sweets and sugar and packets of chai, and a towel for each of us.

All the hubbub and noise of the station mixed with a sustained period of fiddling and adjusting as we fell over and bumped into one another, settling into home for the next several days.

Ours was the last unoccupied cabin in the carriage, so it made sense it was down at the end by the toilet, and Mirja rather liked the idea because it was convenient. And the toilet flushed with water, there was ready cold water in the wash basin, and there was even a roll of toilet paper, at least to start. They scrubbed it down sometimes. It didn't even smell.

The baby next door kept waddling down to peer into our compartment. His parents, bless them, kept the kid quiet.

Everything eventually settled out and darkness came up to close around the Rossiya as we moved east of E-kat, in the rain.

•••••

Movement and noise, action and business at every stop. Traders crowded under the lights with food, furs and shawls. The Europeans and Americans popped onto the platform to stretch and take videos of the locals, and the wheels were checked and the kiosks thrived (and they were well-provisioned) and then the Rossiya groaned back to life and pulled away, and everything aboard settled back into the torpor induced by the rhythm of the rails.

I slept from 1:00 a.m. and as I drifted in and out I saw Mirja sitting by the window gazing out at the countryside far into Siberia. The clouds pulled back, because later you could see that somewhere there was a moon. By 5:00 I was ready for coffee and sunrise but Mirja wanted darkness for a little while more, and I fell right back and slept until 10:00.

You could wash your hair in the wash basin if you had a sink stopper, and even feel positively fresh in the morning, as pale blue sky, high, benign clouds and beautiful white birch trunks rolled by. Shrubs and some of the smaller trees were giving over to yellow leaves.

During the night we'd stopped at Tyumen and Omsk, and by now we'd entered a region a hundred kilometers from Kazakhstan called the Baraba steppe.

The guide book: "It appears as if there is a continuous forest in the distance." Right about that, so it does....

"However if you walk towards it you will never get there as what you are seeing are clumps of birches and aspen trees that are spaced several kilometers apart. The lack of landmarks in this area has claimed hundreds of lives." The Baraba steppe extends 600 kilometers.

Barabinsk train station.

By afternoon we'd reached Barabinsk (population 36,000), 1222 kilometers east of Ekaterinburg, founded a hundred plus years ago around the construction of the railroad, which curiously missed the older town of Kuibyshev, in view in the distance to the north.

Must've been 68 or 70 degrees, perfect air, as we all clambered out to stretch. They sold tons of some particular flayed and dried fish. The good people of Barabinsk still looked thoroughly European, not a bit Asian.

Alongside the rails, cabbages stood ready for picking and there were acres of sunflowers, but everything - plants, people, stray dogs - clung tight to civilization as represented by the rail line. Beyond lay nothing. We never saw a tarmac road between Ekaterinburg and Novosibirsk, over 2500 kilometers.

East of Barabinsk a particular aquamarine colored paint took hold of all the buildings. Siberian Green. The sky settled into a deep blue with puffy clouds, the kind of pollution-free weather you don't get anymore back home.

The dining car menu spoke four languages, using "mith" for "with," as a sensible cross between the English "with" and the German "mit." On the theory that they can't hurt you with soup, we enjoyed chicken noodle. The whole dining car smelled like last night's party. Old beer and cigarettes.

The idea of keeping up with the hours fell away. The timetable showed local time and Moscow time, and we were either fifty minutes early or four hours ten minutes late, take your pick, at the next stop.

The sun slanted in as the Rossiya chugged into and out of the biggest city in Siberia, Novosibirsk, at 1.6 million, here solely because of the construction of the Ob River railroad bridge. In Novosibirsk boulevards were made of real tarmac. There was said to be an enormous opera house, and somewhere nearby was the purpose-built city of Akademgorodok – a city of scientists.

Housing blocks stretched out, too many to count. Since this was a mere settlement in Czarist times, and didn't really get going until Stalinism was the style, Novosibirsk was just flat plug ugly.

Out on the platform, Roma beggars displayed whining snotty children as evidence they were miserable.

•••••

Sunflowers hung their heads with nowhere to point. Pumpkins lay on the vine alongside the cabbage fields. All the hay was cut and piled in heaps tall as houses. Smoke rose above a few chimneys, but the temperature was bracing, and in light of the months to come you'd think they wouldn't bother with fires.

It was morning, early, barely six, but already the villages stirred, those that rose up the rainy hillsides outside Krasnoyarsk. Children played on the gravel track.

A man all in gray, smoking, walked a sodden path, coat flapping at his flanks - a scene that could have taken place in the last century – or the one before that. From compartment nine Mirja and I took it all in – the mists in the trees, the elderly people clustered at the storefront door, the birches steadily losing their autumn fight, the smoke rising from this odd shack or that.

A battleship gray sky defined the whole world.

The Rossiya crossed the mighty River Yenisei, that rises in Mongolia, bisects Siberia, and means "wide river" in the local Evenki language. The Yenisei waterway energizes Krasnoyarsk industry, and the bridge across it brought a dramatic start to our day, as the clack-clacking sound of crossing the bridge jolted us awake. The train was still quiet as Mirja and I took drinks from the samovar.

She drank the chai provided in a heavy glass mug she got from the provodnitsa (whose name was Lydia Ivanova), and I, rather less in harmony with my surroundings, enjoyed Eight O'Clock brand instant coffee in my Evernew brand silver titanium 400 mug.

In Greenland, each settlement presents its worst side to arriving visitors. Since the only contact there is by sea, your arrival by boat is met by benzene storage tanks and refuse waiting to be hauled away. There was a little of that first-things-first frontier utilitarianism in these villages, too.

Giant metal gantries extended the power grid right straight over and through residential areas, and a hundred TV antennas sprouted, and then over time listed randomly over the rooftops.

After Novosibirsk, especially east of the River Yenisei, the Rossiya would crest a hill and we'd stare down at birch and aspen forest as far as the eye could see, broken sometimes by patches logged for firewood.

In valleys the sky was slate. Only from hilltops might you peek at distant pale blue, which might foreshadow improving weather in the afternoon – or might not.

•••••

By now it was easy to spend hours between stops in a dreamy half-consciousness – just be still and the movement of the train would do the work of the hypnotist's pocket watch. Over the course of the week I dipped in and out of epic dreams starring everyone I'd ever known and featuring vague, unfulfilled intimations of desperate evil.

The hypnosis of the rails made travel across the taiga deeply restful. Hours slipped happily by. I imagined that in winter, with the darkness, that would be all the more true.

Kilometer 4375, Ilanskaya. Twenty minute stop. It felt good to get out of the train and stand in the rain. As you began to miss refrigerated drink, the cure was ice cream from the kiosks. Here, kerchiefed babushkas sold cucumbers from a bowl and the provodnitsa bought carrots. The baby next door was the star of the train and everybody played with him at the stops.

Buying dried fish on the platform.

By a town called Taishet, the music from tinny speakers on the platforms had ceased to be repetitive, cloying Russian pop. It had an Asian, maybe Indian rhythm. The Rossiya didn't stop for long, just three or five minutes.

Taishet was once a gulag transit camp. The factory in Taishet where prisoners once died creosoting railroad ties still operates.

•••••

We planned to leave the train for a few days at Irkutsk, so one morning before her daily vacuuming tour, I visited Lydia Ivanova's provodnitsa den down by the samovar and the drying mushrooms to make sure of our arrival time in Irkutsk. It sure was 2:25 in the morning. I had written "Irkutsk" in Cyrillic on a card and I said "pazhalsta," or please. She smiled and turned away from her gossip magazine. I pointed at the word, my watch, and turned up my palms and shrugged.

She asked, speaking fast Russian and gesturing, "Moscow time or local time?" and since I knew how to say the word Moskva, I chose Moscow time and she clucked "nyet nyet

nyet" and wrote it for me in local time (2:25 a.m.) and then in Moscow time (9:25 p.m.).

•••••

5:00 p.m., Nizhny Udinsk, kilometer 4680: A big stop. Fifteen minutes. The taiga had been running dense and hilly, and Mirja had been reclaiming sleep in bulk.

I shook some instant coffee into my mug and stopped at the samovar by the door. First we were trapped on a narrow siding, then a local train pulled away that opened up a long promenade of kiosks across the tracks.

A whitewashed building painted "toilet" was bigger than most houses, with six multi-paned windows along the side. The usual scruffy commerce went on beside the train, and three girls with high, Asian cheekbones and reddish hair panhandled. Only two, really, and very quietly. The other was too meek.

They were insistent, but not even faintly in the way of the souk, and they slipped away of their own volition just before Lydia Ivanova, Provodnitsa-in-Chief, strode up to shoo them away.

Basic provisions, gossip magazines, a newspaper. Things to pass the time were for sale in the kiosks. And cassettes: bootlegs with typed covers like Captain Jack '97, Dance Rocket Part 2 and Hit Hammer, and several with women in lurid poses.

Gray and chillier now, and for the first time, in patches, the birches were completely yellow.

At dusk, lights glowed from inside the old wooden Siberian houses and smoke rose straight into the air from the chimneys. We sat before the window and considered compartment nine in carriage seven of train number two our own personal traveling theatre.

Typical house along the rail line.

The mist-green of the taiga and the soldier-blue sky merged in the fading light, and the light in the compartment reflected on the glass an image of the accumulated odds and ends of travel: Ms. Ivanova's heavy, stout glass, chai bags and books and sugar cubes. Reading glasses and a roll of tissue, hot sauce and a plate and aqua minerale. Plastic cutlery and half a pack of raspberry sweet crackers.

Now we were stopped in front of an unlit stretch of track and people bustled about. Someone came and someone went, but it was all in the dark and we couldn't tell. Was it Zima?

No, it was too short a stop. Zima would be more important than that, and then it would be four hours 53 minutes to Irkutsk.

But Zima never came. No cluster of lights ever suggested suburbs, and the Rossiya hurtled on through the dark. So I did the sensible thing. I went to buy some beers.

In the restaurant car, Sasha exuberantly proclaimed our friendship. He sat with the lady in charge. Muscles bulged from his t-shirt, which was inexplicably drenched with sweat. He ordered three bottles of wine for himself. The attendant had to do the invoice on a calculator and in longhand and deliver the bottles before it was my turn, giving Sasha time to uncork and decant a couple of glasses.

"Sasha, Weelyum," he shouted and stuck his finger in our chests. I had a gulp, we professed friendship, and I turned to find every eye in the restaurant car, amused, on me.

I pointed and explained, "Sasha." They smiled and agreed.

Finally it was time to get back to our berth and break out the bags and fuss about, because we'd be getting off the train in four hours, or three, or five.

I am sure only God will ever know why, of all the world's music, Funky Nassau ("Mini-skirts, maxi-skirts, Afro hair DOOs....") ran in a continuous loop through my brain from Krasnoyarsk to Irkutsk.

And then Zima came to us as a slight strip of concrete between two trains populated by smoking Siberians, and nothing more.

The night provodnitsa said it was ten till seven Moscow time. According to Lydia Ivanova, day provodnitsa (who must have been kicking up her heels at this hour in the provodnitsa lounge), arrival in Irkutsk was expected at 9:25 Moscow, 2:25 Irkutsk.

• • • • •

At 2:00 I tried the bar car for a last minute take-away pivo. At 2:00 a.m. it was a rockin', smoky, all-Russian party car.

The short-order cook by day ruled tonight, and he rose from beside Ludmyla, his puffy-haired paramour, and wondered what kind of pivo I wanted, starting to tick off Baltica, ... And I said Melnick (which means Miller) and he went to get some.

Ludmyla was convinced I was a secret Russian.

"Russki?"

"Nyet, Amerikanski."

"Russki!" with a wag of a finger and a suggestion that we would all have champanski. But by now we were minutes from arrival in Irkutsk.

I paid the smiling short-order cook and smelled like a smoking factory as I bumped back down the corridor, and I got in the way of a woman entering the toilet. She stepped back - in her nightie - with her husband.

Flustered, I summoned the Russian "Spaseba," and she replied, "Not at all" in flawless English.

●●●●●

6 BURMA

Aye Chan Zin, a 22 year old competitive bicycle racer, once raced from Rangoon to Mandalay and back. He fell and lost both incisors to gold teeth.

"Road very bad out there," he grinned, goldly.

Aye Chan ("EEE-Chan,") was a kid of relative privilege, a third-year vet school student with parents with government jobs. His dad was Chinese, a doctor working in Burma on a leprosy project. His mom was a philosophy teacher at Yangon University. A family album he kept in the car was chock full of smiling brothers and sisters.

He had his Dad's tan Toyota with tinted windows. We hired him as our driver, and on Tuesday the seventh of February or, as The New Light of Myanmar newspaper called it, the eighth waxing of Tabodwe, 1356 ME, we set out for a drive into the country.

First on Chan's tour of Rangoon hotspots, "That's military headquarters."

Did the leadership live there?

"Not live just work."

There was the parliament building far across a lawn. It was not possible to visit the parliament building. You can tour the White House, the Kremlin, the Great Hall of the People, but not the Myanmar parliament. Up next came Myanmar Television and Radio, and then, "ice factory."

Guides have their peculiarities. A man we once hired in Beijing forever wanted to try out his English.

"That is tree. Tree?" Zhong from Beijing would ask.

Here in Burma, Chan was factory infatuated. Before the end of the day we saw: ice factory, milk factory, brick factory ("you want to take picture?"), rice factory and garment factory.

Past the Rangoon airport the road opened up to become almost African. An atrocious broken asphalt, open spaces, people with baskets on their heads, most of them barefoot.

Houses were thatch. Ladies raised parasols against the sun (although that was most un-African).

On the road in Burma.

At the World War II allied cemetery, the names of all 27,000 war dead under British crown command in the British Burma and Assam campaigns were inscribed in stone alongside long, well-manicured rows of graves. Names like Wrigley and Hicks, Collins and Stark, and also Singh and Gurung and Pun.

The road remained "under renovation" all the way to Bago, and the whole local population was at work on the job. Barefoot women carried rocks in wicker baskets on their heads for crushing by big rolling machines.

Road work conscripts made 100 kyats ("chots") a day for six hours of carrying rocks on their heads, with a meal included. That's a dollar. We read before we left of a similar project up in Mandalay where the public was used to build infrastructure for no pay.

Once we made friends with a couple named Agron and Besa, on a trip to Albania. This road work made us think of a program Besa described from her childhood under Albania's dictator Enver Hoxha, called the Albanian Revolutionary Triangle, which included physical labor as part of schooling.

But in Burma, pagodas dotted the horizon like the concrete military pillboxes Hoxha scattered across the Albanian countryside. And there was not a single military or para-military or teens-on-the-prowl-for-extorted-cigarettes roadblock. Not one.

People really lived outdoors more than in in Burma. Thatch and open rooms. It was the vast Mississippi flood plain with banana trees.

Out in the middle of rubber farms in the middle of nowhere, we were cruising along dodging the roadwork when suddenly, just before noon, the world exploded before us.

The whole earth went splintery and kaleidoscopic with a terrific bang.

Chan kept his heavy foot on the gas for four or seven seconds, the tan Toyota flew down the road, and all three of us were blinded until slowly we realized the windshield had busted. We couldn't see a thing in the billowing dust and finally Chan coasted to a halt.

He anguished for a time. He wanted to be alone. There'd be hell to pay for busting his Dad's windshield. Mirja and I walked over to the roadside to let him grieve. He pulled some of the big glass chunks out of the windshield and I got up and helped, both of us cutting our hands a little and scraping the glass off the seats and wiping the sweat off our brows. A bird cawed a curious tune. Two men wandered out to look.

There was no choice but to bounce on the last 25 minutes to Bago. Little by little, shards and chunks fell from the windshield frame and they flew, along with the dust and never-before-emission-inspected exhaust, straight into our faces.

And so we limped ahead to Shwemawdaw Pagoda. It's true – Burma means lurching from pagoda to pagoda, and now we came face to face with the "Great Golden God" pagoda. It was taller than the Shwedagon, the dominant pagoda at Rangoon, they said, but it was deserted on this day, which was good for dusting up the bottoms of your feet for a walk around.

An earthquake in 1917 sent the top of this thing tumbling. Enterprising little cusses built a small pagoda right on top of the fallen portion at the base of the big pagoda and put up a sign commemorating the event.

Teak and Jasmine trees dropped ivory blossoms before us. There were tablets of stone that they said predated Buddhism. Competing Buddhist evangels shouted into microphones soliciting money for improvements, which was just about as bizarre as you'll see. One little independent fellow farther down the road just solicited in general, under a revival tent that would do a southern Baptist proud.

A musty amusement park atmosphere held sway in a languorous, sleepy way, with little gaily colored pavilions ringing the main pagoda like the different countries' pavilions around a really tiny Epcot Center. All of them were different.

The monastery next door revealed a portrait of Buddhists as pack rats - eight zillion little icons of Buddhas and pagodas occupied every inch of space. Seemed to me the impact of any one was diminished by being surrounded by so many others. The more the merrier, I guess.

The holy word had been inscribed on long stacks of leaves - for centuries, I guess. Monks' austere sleeping rolls, and a wood floor, comprised their quarters. Kids chiseled new wood adornments for the grounds. A woman sauntered by offering watermelon - by the slice, pre-sliced - from a tray on her head. And chomping on one herself.

•••••

Chan decided, yep, his Dad was gonna kill him. His only hope - stay with a friend and work all night to figure out how to fix the windshield. Said he knew a guy with a glass shop.

We studied his passport at lunch (AHA! We KNEW he was privileged - he had a passport). Never been abroad - a lifelong Rangooner - but he could!

It said born 13 May 1973. It said he was authorized to travel to Singapore, Malaysia, Thailand and Italy (?). And it said, "This passport must be surrendered by bearer upon re-entry into Union of Myanmar."

•••••

Back in Rangoon, Chan turned down University Avenue. This was where Aung San Suu Kyi lived, behind a yellow and green picket fence at #54. She's the daughter of the national hero Aung San, and her National League for Democracy was freely elected in 1990. The State Law and Order Restoration Council, or SLORC, admitted the results but wouldn't hand over power.

But to say "freely elected" is misleading. In the run-up to the election whole towns were dislocated, as we'll see, in an attempt to un-track the Aung San Suu Kyi steamroller. Even through all this, NLD won convincingly. So now instead of fleeing to join her husband in London with the certainty that she could never return, Aung San Suu Kyi lived alone, surrounded by military at #54 University Avenue - across Lake Inya from the military leader.

Chan pointed out there was no military outside.

"Inside the gate," he said.

•••••

Burma was a place that really didn't work too well. It was a backwater - a bustling little backwater, true enough, but just where was it bustling off to?

Driving was on the right, a gift from SLORC, which also changed the name Burma to Myanmar. Britain was the colonial power and left driving was the rule until SLORC woke up insecure one day and decided to reassert control by decreeing that from some date forward driving would be on the right.

Fine. Suddenly, one day to the next, buses dumped their passengers directly into traffic.

•••••

Just before sunset one day I figured out which ferry goes back and forth across the River Yangon and climbed on. Darkness was creeping up.

People stared, but benevolently, and a few approached with halting greetings. "Philip," a seaman, greeted me and told me it was one kyat to do the ferry. So I put some money down and a got a wad of decaying bills back.

The "Autobus 1" had three bare bulbs overhead and a pile of eight-inch tall wooden seats that you grabbed and sat down low on, so I did. Pretty soon I was surrounded by three boys, maybe 17, 15 and eight. Didn't really speak English and I ain't got a lick of Burmese. They just wanted to sit with the foreigner. So we sat and smoked. What the hell.

Maybe 150 people were on board for the eight-minute trip to the village across the way, and maybe 40 people back. After we chugged up to the far side Mr. Eight Year Old and a co-worker gathered the little stools in a big pile for retrieval by the next batch of passengers.

Mr. Fifteen Year Old hopped off the boat and negotiated a Heineken for me from a man with a cooler who sat by the light of two candles on the dock. Directly across the river, line of sight from the downtown of the capital city of Burma, there was no electricity. Just candles.

"How much?" I asked 15.

"95 kyat," he told me, but he wouldn't let me pay. "Present," he said.

Ad exec, Rangoon.

Alongside the Sule Pagoda in Rangoon, a sheet draped over an awning displayed pins and icons in the national colors: green for agriculture and white for purity. Alongside them were piles of green and white plastic tags with Burmese writing.

Were these name tags? They were. Can you do my name, in Burmese? We can.

So U Bo Gyi took my order. I spelled out "Bill" and "Mirja" onto his pad and he painstakingly wrote these in Burmese characters. He handed his work off to the craftsman two booths down, whom I came to know over the next day as (Can you beat this name?) Mg Ko Oo. Pronounce that, roughly, mond-kuh-oooo.

This slender, tiny guy worked his art like a science. With a razor blade he cut the hard plastic strips to length. Out of a wooden box he pulled a round, flat base maybe two inches tall. On this he placed the plastic strip.

He brought his wire-rimmed glasses down four inches from the working surface and peered intently ahead. With an awl he carefully chiseled the circular Burmese letters from the plastic by turning the name tag away, then back in circles round the base.

He rubbed a grease pencil hard over the grooves to make the letters white, then wiped away the excess with a cloth and brought out sandpaper to smooth the sides of the plastic. A bit more plastic, a safety pin, and a spot of glue - kept in a "Burplex vitamin B" bottle, and your name tag was done. Two for a dollar.

I left an order for more with all my friends' names.

•••••

Chan was back the next day as our driver and brought Kyaw Win Maung, who came along to tell us what was what - for fifteen dollars. I rushed outside and around the corner and found that Chan had by God (Buddha?) done it! Between 6:00 p.m. and 10:00 a.m. Chan had got a brand new Toyota windshield installed. In Burma!

He didn't understand high-fives, but backslapping was good enough.

"How did you do it?"

"My friend has a glass shop," he grinned. "We finished last night nine o'clock."

This was the greatest news. His Dad wouldn't kill him.

The plan was to get out on the Irrawaddy, and Chan headed for the lower Pazundaung jetty while we got to know Kyaw Win Maung (call him "Chaw").

Kyaw finished school in '77 as a geologist but had always been a tour guide. Clear-eyed and soft-spoken with an open face, Kyaw was easy to like, and it didn't take much prodding to hear his whole story.

When he first started his tour guide job he was posted to Pagan, optimistically eight hours drive to the northwest and full of ancient pagodas.

He met and married a country girl, built a house himself, and settled back, he thought, to live out his life there. The sunsets were beautiful, he smiled. They had a daughter.

Then a man he'd met in his tour guide job invited him to visit the U.S. After saving enough to care for his family while he was away, off he went. For six months he stayed in the U.S. He saw his first snow in Carlisle, Pennsylvania.

One day in 1988 he heard on Christian Science Monitor radio that his entire village had to move. The military government was trying to disrupt the elections in March of that year.

A week later he got a letter from his wife saying she had a week to tear down the house he'd built and move, along with everybody else in town, ten kilometers away.

He went back to Burma, gathered his wife and baby and moved in with his father in Rangoon. His brother died at 32 leaving two nieces for Kyaw to care for today, along with his wife, daughter and now, his elderly dad too.

His wife was a simple country girl. She had a small business selling candy to kids, cheroots, that kind of thing, when they met in Pagan and he didn't know how she'd do in the big city. So although he hoped to visit the U.S. again and had a standing invitation from his Pennsylvania friend, it would be some time before he got his nieces off to college and saved enough (at $15 a day) to provide for his dad, wife and child in his absence.

It was a longyi day. The day before Chan had been in pants, but today both Chan and Kyaw wore their traditional longyis, which are colored cloths worn as a sort of skirt by both sexes. They wear 'em from here west to India, but as Kyaw explained, they're "long - yee's" here, "lon - gee's" in India.

Kyaw had chosen a black and white print, and Chan looked elegant in a regal sort of gold and purple thing. At the bottom of each, hairy legs and thongs finished off the look.

In the morning the BBC reported on the hotel TV that Burma had released 20 NLD political prisoners. Kyaw said it wasn't on Myanmar TV, but that wasn't surprising, since SLORC denies holding any political prisoners.

Myanmar TV was one station. There was nothing else on the dial. Nothing. It broadcast a few hours in the evening, a few in the morning, too, and on weekends. Here's a schedule from the New Light of Myanmar:

View Today:
Friday (10-2-95)

5:00 pm
1. Martial music
5:20 pm
2. Disco Rally
5:40 pm
3. Songs of National Races
6:00 pm
4. Traditional Food of National Races
(Domestic Training School)
(Rakhine)
6:15 pm
5. Songs of Yester Year
7:00 pm
6. Children's programme
7:15 pm
7. Programme honouring the 48th Anniversary of the Union Day
7:30 pm
8. Agricultural Force - Country's Development
7:40 pm

9. Programme honouring the 48th Anniversary of the Union Day
7:45 pm
10. Beauty of the State, Dances of the State
7:50 pm
11. Songs in honour of the National Convention
8:00 pm
12. News
13. (something in Burmese - ?)
14. International news
15. National news
16. Weather report
17. Programme honouring the 48th Anniversary of the Union Day (something in Burmese - ?)
18. The next day's programme

•••••

The Yangon - Thalyin bridge was three two-and-a-half kilometer, Chinese-built lanes - one paved each way and a rail track separating them in the middle. Having just one lane on a bridge doesn't keep anybody from passing, of course.

From China all the way around southeast Asia to here, the technique for driving is always the same: If you get out around the car in front of you fast enough, you present the oncoming drivers with a fait accompli: I am tying up the entire highway in front of you, so you have no choice but to brake and let me merge in front of the guy beside me.

Naturally the oncoming traffic plots to do the same. Seldom is there tranquility on the highways of Southeast Asia.

And amidst it all, whole Burmese families plodded by on ox cart or old blue Ford or Dodge "buscars" with men and boys stuffed everywhere inside, standing hanging on the back, and a dozen more piled on top. Invariably they all broke into wide smiles and waved madly as they plodded past.

A grizzled brown field worker walked out of a brilliant yellow-green paddy to trade some greens ("grass for soup") and two watermelons for one of Chan's Lucky Strikes. Here they had "brick factory," "rice factory" and "vegetable factory."

And more road work. The guys with the machines – it was their job. The conscripts - they got their 100 kyats a day and lunch. Yummy.

At Kyauk Tan village you hopped a little wooden dinghy over to the floating pagoda. They said it had never flooded and was thereby proof of the auspiciousness of the Buddha. People made pilgrimages for their "economy," or financial health.

There were these three rocks on stools, see, and if you picked up the green one on the right and it felt light, that was auspicious for your economy. It felt pretty light to me, which was good, because we were going to need some auspicious economy when we got home.

A vivid belief in spirits thrived in Burma. Kyaw gave a go at explaining the curious mix of animism and Buddhism. Banyan trees, for example, are known to have spirits. Wherever you find a banyan tree, chances are you'll find a spirit house underneath it. It's just a little wood box with an open front. Inside you place bananas or pomilons or some other offering to the spirits.

So what happened when there was a banyan tree at a pagoda? No problem. You got a spirit house in the middle of Buddha's house. There was no conflict. Both belief systems were intertwined.

There is the story of a particular banyan tree on the Bago road, just before the British cemetery. The shamans under this tree blessed cars. New car owners moved their cars forward and back three times as if bowing to the car spirit in the banyan tree. Some people got a little insurance blessing each time they drove by. And who knows? We hadn't stopped and an hour later we didn't have a windshield.

Down at the water's edge beside the Floating Pagoda, fat catfish jostled one another for food the kids threw into the water. We took a spin out around the river, then a walk around Kyauk Tan village.

Nasty nasty nasty dried fish were for sale on a table. At the end of the street, a house that was the town theatre screened Burmese videos twice a day, five kyats. The people out here in the country liked Burmese tear jerkers, Kyaw said. In the big city smuggled videos from Thailand were all the rage.

Kyaw reckoned they came over concealed amid legal goods in trucks. They were strictly illegal. The government sanctioned only good ol' Burmese entertainment.

On videotapes smuggled into Burma you didn't get subtitles. That's why Chuck Norris and Rambo were so big. It had to be action because they didn't understand the words.

A guy made tin pots by an ancient method involving spinning a wheel that I just didn't understand. One girl just stopped dead in her tracks and stared at us, holding a watermelon slice from the tray on her head. Machines ground sugar cane into a sugary drink.

We drove over to the dock. Chan bought some betel in an unspeakably filthy wood hut they called the waiting room. The betel leaf in Burma is green, wide and round. They slathered it with paste and sprinkled a few betel nut pieces on top. The paste and nuts are bitter. They're for calcium. The leaf is a mild amphetamine.

You could buy branches too, inside of which some God-forsaken larvae nestled. Yep, you bought the branch, plucked the thing out and popped it in your mouth. Tasted like butter, Kyaw said, except crunchy. This was more of a Chinese practice than a Burmese one, he assured us, and he'd only tried it once.

My God, these people were eating worms out of trees!!!

The boat wasn't due until 4:00, it was 2:30 and evil hot, so we drove home and never got the boat ride we set out for.

The river near Kyauk Tan.

In the main hall of the international airport assembly area were five wall clocks. It was a quarter of six in Hong Kong, a quarter of six in Singapore, a quarter of five in Bangkok, a quarter of ten in the morning GMT - and four fifteen in Burma.

At the top of the stairs the dark glass door reading "Thai Air" swung open. Three hostesses were wedged between the open door and a wall, smiling welcome. We squeezed past them into a minuscule dark room with three couches. Two were taken, so we put our stuff down and sat on the other, sort of between the lounge and the hallway.

"Hello sir. Would you like Pepsi, 7 Up, coffee, tea?" Dazzling smiles.

"Well, how about a beer?"

"No beer."

Stifled grins from the couples on the couches in the dark.

"Oh...ok."

"Sir outside you can buy beer and bring back here. Cost five dollars," she smiled through the darkness.

"Good price," I remarked.

"Yes sir," brightly.

"Well, okay, you have Pepsi."

"Yes sir!"

"Do you have that in a can? Can I have a can of Pepsi?"

"No sir."

Bright teeth shone.

"Well, what do you have it in?"

"Pepsi, 7 Up, coffee, tea."

"Do you have water?" Mirja tried.

"No ma'am, no water. Pepsi, 7 Up ...."

We opted for five dollar beers down at the bar, and squeezed past two new guys waddling down the entrance way. Wished 'em well.

"Five dollars is a lot for a Heineken, eh?" I asked our big ol' waitress.

She shook her head and clucked, "Government price."

Jammed thick onto the viewing platform, families craned and waved at kin walking up the Silk Air ramp, Singapore bound, probably on the first flight of their lives, craning and waving madly back.

Poignant. You couldn't really afford to fly if you were common folk and we couldn't help but think they had saved and saved for those tickets, and maybe the fervent waves were because some of those guys weren't coming back.

●●●●●

7 CHILEAN PATAGONIA

A band of cold rain swept over the Hotel Cabo de Hornos, churning the Strait of Magellan dirty gray. Punta Arenas's "oldest and grandest" hotel was, well, it was just a hotel, all of its walls painted a determined shade of mustard. A bare minimum of staff kept the Cabo de Hornos open and we all watched cold squalls spray over the strait.

The Pan American highway stops at Puerto Montt, 816 miles of Chilean coastline to the north, so there are no roads here. There is little tourism. You have to be damned determined to get here.

Feliz Navidad. Punta Arenas was closed tight, for we came in on Christmas night.

•••••

I think I snared the last car for rent in southern Chile.

I bought coffee and stopped on the plaza to rub the shiny toe of a statue of Magellan, then I found Hertz.

"Buenos dias. You have a car?"

"No."

A happy smile.

"If I go to aeropuerto?"

"No."

I looked across the street. "Budget?"

This "no" betrayed a smug certainty, and at the same time a creeping regret that he wasn't helping. He allowed that I could always "ask the question" across the street at Budget and furthermore, the man down the street at Santander might have uno auto. He wouldn't open until ten and it was only 9:30. Still, that was something, so I bid him and another man who was washing cars adios.

At Budget they had big smiles but no cars.

"For today!?" He acted amazed.

He phoned around, but nothing. At least I had "asked the question."

•••••

It's hard to imagine that the nearly Antarctic tip of South America came to be known as Tierra del Fuego, or land of fire. It's likewise hard to imagine being so far from home – so isolated – as Ferdinand Magellan and his crew were, sailing through appalling weather where nobody they'd ever heard of had been, five centuries ago. Especially when they spotted huge bonfires onshore.

Tribes called Ona and Yaghan kept fires constantly stoked for warmth. The Yaghan wore only the scantest clothing despite the cold. They smeared seal fat over their bodies to fend off the wind and rain.

Canoeists, adept at navigating the labyrinthine channels and tributaries around the straits, they hunted the sea. Between Magellan in 1520 and Charles Darwin on the H.M.S. Beagle in 1834, not a lot changed. Darwin noted "these people going about naked and barefoot on the snow."

The Ona lived across the strait, on the island I could just see through the spray and mist. The books call them fierce warriors who adorned themselves with necklaces of bone, shell and tendon, and who, wearing heavy furs and leather shoes, intimidated the bare-skinned Yaghan. Darwin gave them their backhanded due, calling them "wretched lords of this wretched land."

An early European settler described life hereabouts as 65 unpleasant days per year complimented by 300 days of rain and storms.

•••••

With time to kill, I walked to the water, stepping lightly past mongrels at a Purina warehouse, and I put my hand in the chilly Strait of Magellan - right there amid a bunch of floating plastic bags and candy wrappers.

One passenger ship was calling just now. Across the strait, looking just about west to east, low hills rose around a town called Porvenir (Future), Tierra Del Fuego. It wasn't very far but I couldn't make it out.

At 10:00 I tried the knob at the Santander Car Rental but it wouldn't turn. The windows were still boarded. Oops, wait a minute. Soon as I turned the knob a man appeared from six doors down and opened the store and ushered me in. The long and short of it (mostly long, since we did the whole mileage and insurance wrangle without a common language) was that I got the last car he had and eventually it appeared, driven by the man who an hour ago had been washing the cars at Hertz.

•••••

Punta Arenas, at 110,000 people, is a proper town with a proper town park, which is home to the statue of Magellan and its smooth, often-rubbed toe. If you rub the toe you'll be sure to come back. Twenty two hundred kilometers south of Santiago, you take what entertainment you get.

Having rubbed the toe we were free to drive, so we set out in our petite white Nissan Saloon to cross 430 kilometers of gravelly wilderness. A wire screen over the windshield served to prevent a crack from gravel flying off the road, the rental car man said. But no other cars had one, so we were embarrassed. Maybe it really was the last car for rent in town.

We looked silly, I thought, motoring off toward the hills. A quarter inch mesh of expanded metal surrounded the window all around. It extended far enough from the windshield for the wipers to operate underneath. A foot-square hole was cut in front of both the driver and the passenger with more mesh hinged over it so that the normal position was open from the top, for city driving, but for your serious gravel roads you could pull a string that reached inside your side window and roll the window up real fast to catch the string and bring the panel down. That sealed the whole windshield against rocks and provided you with about a thirty percent view of the world in front of you.

•••••

A hundred kilometers of blacktop, virtually no houses, virtually no traffic. A little bit of Greenland, with tiny white wildflowers but no trees. Then the pavement disappeared, a Mack truck barreled by, and we battened down the wire hatches.

Eventually intermittent rain, lack of traffic and squinty tension convinced us we really didn't need the mesh pulled down. A few other cars had wire cages, but not most, and we made it all the way without a crack. At one point it was one paved lane for eighty kilometers.

At a place called Reubens, where stood a settlement of a few buildings, there began to be trees again. The Nire, or Notofagus antarctica, the native species, grows to twenty crooked and branched meters, compacted and dominated by the winds. Fields of tree trunks stood twisted and contorted by wind. The forest was two colors of green - the needles and lighter clinging lichen.

Rolling hills replaced the horizon-to-horizon flat. You could watch sheets of rain approach from miles away and wash overhead on their march to the other horizon.

260 kilometers up the road we refueled at Puerto Natales, the last town. Slung over low hills, it overlooked a bay from which ships sailed up to the Torres del Paine park, and there was a nice view across the harbor to snow capped mountains.

Tarmac surrounded Puerto Natales, but gravel returned minutes outside of town, for the last long 130 kilometers plus 58 additional kilometers we'd find out about later.

Snow topped a few low peaks.

Sheep on their way to Estancia Domingo

A thousand sheep blocked the road. Two gauchos and a squad of dogs marched them forward. The dogs ran and darted, responding to the gauchos' whistles, and moved the sheep off the road for us. Mirja pointed out they weren't sheepdogs, but mutts, or "cocktail dogs" as she put it, and observed that you wouldn't need to play with these dogs at night because they'd be worn out.

They, and we, were bound for a place called Estancia Domingo (Domingo's ranch). Over a rise beyond it, like flipping a switch, the horizon suddenly revealed a snow-covered massif that made us exclaim.

There were big birds about, but neither condors, with their white collars, nor the nandu, said to look like a feather duster. At a fork where a sign pointed toward "administración," a series of lakes, ups and downs and curves began, and Mirja spotted guanacos. Herbivores, they live all over the park, usually grazing like mountain goats in steep cliff areas.

They're maybe four feet tall at the shoulders, llama-like, brown and white, from the camel family. They may weigh 200 pounds. They live in family groups, and we usually saw them with their kids. They'd do this funky juke with their long necks when they ran.

Park administración noted our arrival in a tatty old book, took some pesos and showed us we still had some 58 kilometers to go. Unfazed anymore by flying gravel and tired of driving, we sped on.

•••••

The Torres del Paine

A long sand spit stretched outside our window at the Hosteria Lago Gray, just in front of the lake. Icebergs floated near shore, not quite building sized, but several people tall. Then in the distance, and not that far in the distance, a massive glacier some hundreds of feet high formed the horizon where it slid down between peaks.

All the peaks were covered with snow, but the ones in the east were taller. In the southern hemisphere, the south face never gets sun, and wide swathes of permanent snowfields gathered in the folds of all the mountains.

Still farther east stood the famous Torres, or Towers, del Paine, and we could see a couple of the Cuernos, or horns, too. They were just impossibly thin, tall formations, jutting so shear that the last of them wasn't scaled until 1963.

Most often they stayed in the clouds, and we only saw them that first day when the light began to fade, maybe past ten. Prevailing wind whipped straight down the glacier north to south, and the trees were all permanently bent to show it.

Mirja and I couldn't remember a windier place. Every night about five or six, it kicked up a gale and bore down, and rattled the windows and whistled through the grass.

•••••

There were frequent jets, and I was befuddled. Over the course of a day I heard six. This was a remote part of the planet, not really between anywhere and anywhere else. Could have been three round trips between Punta Arenas and the populated part of Chile, I guessed, but I doubted it.

There was a flight a week to Islas Malvinas, or the Falkland Islands, but that was Wednesdays and this was Sunday, so maybe they were flying to Antarctica, where Chile claims thirty million cubic kilometers of ice. Never figured it out.

•••••

We set out over a suspension bridge ("2 max at a time") and along the edge of Lago Gray to see the icebergs, bluer by degrees than the water, then up to Mirador (lookout) Ferrier - a vertical rise of just 300 meters, but as steep and tough as we wanted.

Gales blew hard across barren rock at the top, with views back west to another snowy peak, and up into Lago Pingo and the glacier at its north end, closer to the Patagonian ice cap.

No wildlife, save for tiny birds. Rabbit sign, though. There were lots of flowers Mirja recognized from Finland, and scrub reached knee high. The clean, clear water we drank from a brook tasted magnificent.

Many dead tree trunks were hollowed and burned, suggesting lightning strikes. Looked like if you were a tree, your life was just to stand around contorting in the wind until eventually you were struck down by lightning.

We left early in the morning and walked back into the lodge late in the day and just like Mirja's cocktail dogs, you wouldn't have to play with us that night.

•••••

One day was heavy and wet, as if a Georgia spring shower might start anytime. By 5:00 we were beset by gray - no Torres showing. Our whole stay in Patagonia it rained nearly the entire time, including from a clear blue sky, but most of the time it rained about three drops per second per square meter. You'd get hit but you'd dry by the time you got out your parka.

We drove a short distance to a car park to hike to Salto (waterfall) Grande. The path was thick with bugs and heavy with wet, but the bugs weren't really after us. The bushes sent out a pungent but pleasant smell either side of the path that was cut flat as if by a foot-wide mower.

Salto Grande, chalky water rushing from Lago Nordenskjöld into Lago Pehoe, wasn't really all that grande, but up and over the hill, suddenly the rumble of the salto gave way to the silent stone face of the Cuerno Principal (2600 meters), the highest of the Cuernos del Paine.

After an hours' walk, Mirja and I stood at the Mirador Nordenskjöld and gazed across Lago Nordenskjöld at Cuerno

Principal, shortly before the clouds conquered the tops of the cuernos for the day.

•••••

At the Posada Serrano, a provisioner along the road back, they were so happy to see us they fried up some fresh papas fritas, so we bought a twelve pack and sat right there and drank most of them with a giant man whose father from Poland and mother from Odessa met in Palęstine and moved to Brazil.

Everyone told stories and passed the time with warm Austral beers right from the box (and french fries) there in the Posada Serrano dining room, cozy and dry in the rain. A happy bonus: there was no one to drive into out there alone on the gravel, driving home in the rain after a six-pack apiece.

•••••

I peered through the Hosteria's front window. As we feared. The common room was filled to the rim with ill-matched groups of families and acquaintances, lining the walls in chairs, waiting to be fed. Every time we ever went inside they alternated two CD's: Pachelbel's Canon and a cheap Out of Africa knock-off. Over and over and over for days.

Hosteria Lago Gray was four-unit prefab blocks with siding, five of them facing one another with driftwood placed deftly in between. The dining room - and this was the only place you could eat for miles around - had ample seating. The common area, alas, was sadly lacking, too small by half, so any one group could dominate.

Instead of going inside, we visited with the chef. He threw meat to a nearly domestic fox, which warily came within feet to grab it. The chef whistled for that fox like for a dog. Outside, one happy bird perched behind the common building, worm writhing in its beak. White and black sea birds cruised the icebergs in pairs close to the surface of the water, one of each pair in full throat.

Baby bergs on Lago Gray.

Five hundred meters across the water at the close end of the sand bar sat the hosteria's low red boat. It looked like holding maybe forty - so it must have been an attraction park-wide, carrying passengers through the bergs up to Glacier Gray.

It was parked now, though, grounded up against a bergy bit. The hosteria, or the captain at least, was being punished for sailing too close to the bergs.

•••••

The Alps are massive and majestic. The Torres del Paine only reach three thousand something meters versus Mont Blanc's 4260. But the Alps have been domesticated, everywhere you go, all the way up onto the slopes. Cowbells tinkle. Farmers keep track of their livestock. Every village is prim.

It's the vastness around the Torres, the silence. There are no houses, no farms. Land isn't delineated by perpendiculars. No fences to keep anything in or out. Nothing, except for the snow and the big rocks, and the water and the animals and the silence. That's what you're after in a place like this, but too often you find yourself in the common room with strangers, hearing about things like Kurt's blister.

"It's out to here," Kurt said several times, showing a distance between his finger and thumb. The wife of Kurt would then chirp something like "He's not very athletic." That was galling because she clearly never auditioned for Buns of Steel.

There are always people like that, though, fighting their petty wars, and Kurt was a good enough old guy, running a party of five, some of them sullen kids.

Maps was what Kurt liked and he'd sink his head deeper into his maps to ignore his wife. The wife of Kurt liked showing people things. She'd go back to the room ("Wait right here," she'd command) to get some page that she'd printed off the internet. Or she'd inflict her sack of trail mix on a very dubious little boy.

Each time she got loud Kurt would move his face closer to his map and trace lines on it with his finger.

The wife of Kurt had a running disagreement with Kurt over the price of gas, or benzene, as they called it here. Kurt had heard they were getting six dollars a litre out of jerrycans back at Posada Serrano and the wife of Kurt wouldn't hear of it.

She worked herself up to high dudgeon (although high is pretty much the only way dudgeon comes) as she asked the dubious little boy's father if he knew the price of benzene, and he allowed that he'd got some and it was close to the normal price.

"See Kurt! Six dollars a litre is impossible! I thought six dollars a litre was impossible. Did you hear that Kurt? I told you six dollars a litre was impossible. Kurt, this man says it's not any six dollars a litre. Kurt thought gas cost six dollars a litre!"

And Kurt pulled the edge of the map nearest his wife nearly to his ear and the little boy's father, who had a naturally puzzled, disheveled look, tried to find somebody else to talk to.

●●●●●

8 GUANGXI PROVINCE, CHINA

Kiosk keepers huddled under strings of bare bulbs. An ancient pagoda perched high up on the hill across the river. Fruit and vegetable vendors and a magazine stand stood open at nine o'clock at night. Around a bend in the road, storefronts set sample dishes on the sidewalk, just out of the rain.

A wet old man beckoned me in. We didn't speak a word in common except "OK" and "bye bye." I drank a couple of big tall green bottles of beer I couldn't read and I bought a bottle of something he thought I should buy. It was some clear elixir he kept pouring and we kept toasting. Mostly we sat in his store and stared into the fog.

•••••

One side of Guilin was shiny, the other just rubble. Five years before, Guilin tore down the buildings on the whole west side of Zhongshan Road and rebuilt them all. Now they were doing the same thing on the east side.

A bed careened by, balanced on a bicycle. Pointy-nosed little three-wheeled machines sputtered along, almost but not quite trucks. Water buffalo halted traffic and chewed the roadside, right in town. Guilin, somehow, was dusty even in the rain.

•••••

Morning came dreary, misty and clammy, with no hope of the weather clearing. We'd arranged a boat trip starting at the nearby town of Zhujiang. Our minder was named Long, our driver was Chang, and our Toyota Crown sedan stifled warm inside.

Speed limit signs hung above the road. To one side was an orange orchard with a collective housing block for the farmers. Close to Zhujiang the pavement turned to six-sided blocks that fit together like the runways at Rinas airport in Tirana, Albania.

That fit. For a time in the 1960's, China was Albania's only ally in the world.

•••••

Two boats idled at the dock - both bright red with yellow trim. Colored dragons stretched the length of each side of the boats.

Inside hung thin orange curtains. Red, blue, pink and yellow bright plastic moulding ringed the cabin, as did multi-colored Christmas lights. A Beijing brand TV stood at the front, hiding our smoking pilot and presenting a videotaped tour in Chinese.

Along each side, seven sets of four by four airline-type seats faced one another with a long wooden table in between each set, topped by a yellow tablecloth on which sat teacups with tops, oranges, hot towels, packages of nuts, a rose in a vase and toothpicks. A cadre of stewardesses served tea, coffee and Tsing Tao beer.

Three smoking Japanese fellows sat across looking back at us as we pulled out into the mist. One owned a shop near Tokyo. He promised our polaroid would hang on the wall of his restaurant.

This guy practiced Chi Kung (or qigong), and had for 20 years. He'd hold his hands around yours, or at your temples and concentrate, and you'd feel hot and begin to tingle. He put his hands on either side of my head and it really worked. Mirja felt it, too.

Roger Pan, beside Mirja in the window seat, was Chinese-Canadian from Toronto. He explained that the symbol "kung" in Chinese means sort of "the art of" and "chi," is loosely "energy."

He estimated that you need to memorize about 5000 Chinese characters to read properly. Since they're characters, not an alphabet in which letters have individual sounds, you can't sound 'em out. You either know 'em or you don't.

Roger was a good kid, vaguely related to then New York Times reporter Sheryl WuDunn. Traveling alone, he'd left his onward air tickets on the seat of a cab somewhere, so he wasn't sure when he could leave.

The Lijiang River (Li) meanders 437 kilometers through Guilin, Yangshuo, Pingle and Wuzhou. Along its banks, famous limestone peaks forever immortalized by Chinese painters rise off the valley floor in the most unlikely shapes.

Clouds played with the tops of the peaks. Standing on the upper deck, I tried to decide whether they were beautiful or just very, very strange. The whole world was muted in mild grays, greens and blues.

The Li River.

The Li ran low and clear enough to see that sometimes it was only three or four feet deep. There was a brisk headwind. On the upper deck you had to turn your collar up and stuff your hands deeper into your pockets.

A billion and a half people in China and nothing on these riverbanks except fishermen and evil, dark cormorants, trained to plunge into the water, grab fish, surface, and spit 'em back at their masters. And one lonely man in a boat, poling along with the current, fishing seaweed from the riverbed.

Working men, in their pointy round straw hats, walked down through rice paddies with poles across their backs supporting two baskets. They piled dirt down at the water's edge.

•••••

Hot pot is sort of a fondue in which lots of raw, formerly-living things are piled around a boiling electric urn and dumped in a little bit at a time. At our table this was handled by a Japanese/Canadian/Finnish committee of five.

Occasionally someone would toss in some bok choy or noodles. Now and then somebody would pluck stuff out with a spoon or chopsticks and chow down. Convivial eating went on for an hour.

The route passed sights such as "five tigers catch a goat," "yearning for husband's return rock," and "an old man push a mill." Later, bamboo began to appear among the Osmanthus trees. Some of it grew to be fist-sized and 30 feet tall.

•••••

It looked like all 20,000 in the village of Yangshuo were bicycling by just as we put out. Chang and his Toyota arrived from Zhujiang. He and Long and Mirja and I packed up and headed back north 80 kilometers to Guilin.

Chang stopped to pay a toll. Long explained, "This is special road from Yangshuo to Guilin."

She was indoctrinated. Went to university at Nanjing. It was easy to get into the language program, she said - lack of demand. So she took English and got her job on graduation. Said she could go abroad, but didn't have the money. Had a nine year old daughter. Mirja asked about the one-child policy.

"People have accepted this."

•••••

Water buffaloes, rice paddies and orange groves passed outside. Roadside stalls peddled identical stacks of pomilons, yellow, big as a grapefruit at the bottom and shaped like a pear. Long said they taste like oranges but "not so juicy."

Guilin farmers still plowed by hand with oxen. Long was disarming: "Almost all farmers have cattle because before they plant they need to plow." Of course.

All manner of two, three and four wheel vehicles traversed the "special road" with us, honking and ringing their bells and spewing exhaust.

China burned cheap coal. You could smell it, and car exhaust, through the walls, on your clothes, everywhere. It was cold and damn wet. There was one time zone in China, Beijing time, and in Guilin it got dark about six o'clock.

Mirja and I bought one of Mao's Little Red Books, dated 1969 with Mao in color, on a Sunday night stroll around town. Took a turn around Elephant Trunk Hill, past an outdoor dance hall and blaring skating rink, and into a department store with escalators up, but not down.

A camera store with Aiwa and Ricoh point and shoots, plus brands like Tomoa, Xinon and Benson, and a huge Yanwu boombox. Dropped a coin in a vending machine, which gave us a calendar with Li Min on the other side. He's a handsome young singer from Hong Kong.

Here at the vending machine we met Li Huan. English student, wanted to practice English, the usual premise, but he was sweet, with bushy thick hair and thick glasses. He lived with his mom and dad in a three room flat. His dad was retired from the local government theatre - had been an artist. He painted scenery for plays.

Li complained about the way you have to buy your way out of the country. He said you had to pay the government 3600 yuan to go to Hong Kong. That was then $437.

Along with Li, we walked in the dark back toward our hotel, down a rough, torn up street. We gave Li 10 yuan to buy a pomilon. They wanted 20 from us. He went alone ahead, got it. Said he talked the vendor down from 16.

Here was a kiosk with snake wine for 60 yuan. The whole snake was inside.

We invited Li in to "Guilin Tea Guiture Association Longlife Tea House." Nobody was there but us. Loud sitar music wailed incongruously. Mirja and I enjoyed Carlsbergs, Li had a Sprite, and the beautiful young waitress with the dazzling smile stood right beside us the whole time we were in there.

•••••

You never know where you are in provincial Chinese cities because there's never a town plan. A warehouse district next door to some food stalls, a wedding dress store, a pool hall, the hospital. Everything's packed so tightly you just roll up and stop, and you hop out because you must be somewhere. Then you find out where you are.

Inside the "Traditional Chinese Medicine Hall of Attached Hospital to Guilin Medical College" a girl in white immediately escorted Mirja, Long and me to seats alone in a dusty lecture room, bare except for tables and chairs, a one-step platform for the teacher, and an anatomy chart in Chinese.

Dr. Mung walked in and Long walked out. Dr. Mung began his traditional medicine lecture, to just the two of us. He traveled elliptically for a while around the basic yin-yang concept, which says yin is blood and yang is energy and the two must be kept in balance and we do this with herbs and acupuncture.

My crest fell (should've fallen sooner) as he passed us a list of 26 pills, liniments and creams available from the Traditional Chinese Medicine Hall, and proceeded to list all 26 from memory, including their indications and usages.

Old Dr. Mung stood there on his step in his dirty white coat with the pullover sweater underneath and showed us the testimonial letters he'd received. The door swung open and two white-coated female assistants carried in a meter-long chain, heated to almost glow.

A wild man followed, touched a scrap of paper to the chain until it went aflame, then intentionally burned the palm of his hand on the chain and in one movement was met by Dr. Mung, who was ready with #8, Cream for Burns and Scalds. He rubbed it into the wild man's palm, even as the wild man reached his seat against the wall opposite the door. All this happened in seconds.

Next Dr. Mung introduced the hospital's Chi Kung expert. The door swung open again. Balls of dust scudded across the medical college's floor. Mr. Expert did some moves to get his electricity centered, plugged in two probes to the 220 volt wall and held 'em.

Dr. Mung held a volt/ohm meter to Mr. Expert at several places and it's needle swung. Mr. Expert was Mr. Electricity. He touched Mirja and me each between our closed eyes and we both could see a flicker of light.

He held either end of the wires to a light bulb and it lit. Now the wild man got up and showed us his palm. The miracle cream had worked. The wild man left.

Mr. Expert now offered us "free treatment" of anything chronic using "bio-electrical acupuncture treatment." So Mirja had her shoulder tension and I had my lower back pain treated, each by our holding one electrical probe, Mr. Expert holding the other and poking the affected areas, causing a tingle.

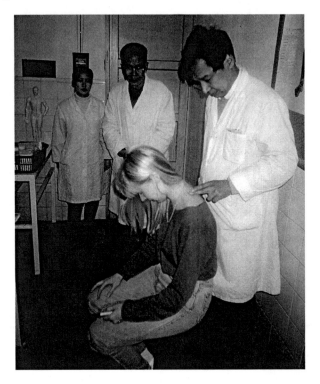

Doctor Mung's clinic.

Now the first girl was back with bottles of pills, #2 and #16 for me, only 100 yuan each for a month's treatment, more for Mirja, putting them in a bag and assuring us, "Credit card is ok."

We left with no pills, creams or liniments, and with Dr. Mung, Mr. Expert and the girl disappointed.

•••••

Fubo hill is one of those karst Guilin oddities, a little round hill that rises out of nowhere. You could easily jog all the way around it in a minute. Mirja and I clambered the 325 steps up and shared a view of Guilin with the gnats.

They'd tell you Guilin was really new to the tourism game - that ten years before it was a backwater. From the top of Fubo Hill, it still was. Gritty, low buildings. Smoke from coal fires. But the surrounding hills, the reason to be in Guilin in the first place, were as compelling and utterly strange as you'll see.

On the last afternoon, still damp and gray and clammy, we set out down the river road toward Fubo hill, then plunged left into the city. Most of the televisions in the stores were black and white. Changan minivans. Liuzhou Disai taxis. One "Za Stava," Russian.

Red is China's national color officially and in fact. Young professional Guilin women would bicycle by, smartly turned out in slacks and a bright red blazer.

You couldn't be the next big-time Chinese tourist town without a gleaming new department store, and the Wang Cheng department store was just that. Here you had escalators that went both up and down. All the mannequins looked Western.

I bought cigarettes to use for tips, fifty cents a pack for Viceroy.

On the street, two students with some English were enchanted by Mirja and eventually persuaded us to their studio ("three minute walk") to meet their teacher. Boy #1 flirted with Mirja. Boy #2 and I walked (not too far) behind.

"What you think of Chinese people?"

"I think Chinese people are happy and they smile a lot."

They agreed but said that was only here in south China. In north China, especially Beijing, they were stoic.

Gravely, boy number two confided, "They're too Communist."

They were art students. Their teacher, in blue-jeans, affable and just a kid, showed us around the studio. Took him six months to paint a six meter scroll of a traditional Chinese scene. His students called him the Picasso of China because of his style, but for sale he painted the Guilin scenes for sale everywhere.

Too bad everybody asked you to buy. In this case the students did the soft-selling, the teacher stayed above the fray, and the prices dropped from the 800 yuan in the art college store to 300.

We found a local bar and sat just inside the door. A young fellow who had good English, Chen, followed us in off the street.

Chen asked us, "Do you want to keep talking to me?"

Such open, unabashed directness. We laughed and told him to pull up a chair.

He helped us order five-Yuan beers (eight was a dollar) in big green, no-name bottles.

The three waitresses stood transfixed before a soap opera that was way too loud. Color TV. Chen said it must have cost 3000 yuan. Typical pay: 600 yuan a month.

He asked us incredulously, he'd heard this somewhere, "In U.S., can you earn four thousand dollars a month?"

I nodded, solemnly.

Chen thought being a doctor wasn't really a great job in China. It paid in the middle. You could really clean up working as an interpreter, taxi driver, in a joint venture, or, the ultimate, as an "individual businessman."

Live fish swam in plastic buckets on the floor by the door. Two foot-tall, owl-like birds called Cat Eyes stared morosely through a cage beside the fish. They were for dinner. Another flapped listlessly on a newspaper on the floor, too near death to get up. The whole thing was wrenching and you wanted to kill the broken one in the name of humanity.

Chen screwed up the courage to ask us to come meet his family, which meant come buy something.

We told him no, but if he wanted to bring something for us to see we'd wait fifteen minutes. He came back with a "gift" of calligraphy he said he'd painted himself. He translated it for us and I immediately forgot.

It just so happened this "gift" was rolled into a scroll containing an ink-on-rice-paper painting of Guilin scenery which he said he'd painted himself and suggested that some people would pay 300 yuan for it.

I told him no.

He asked if we'd like to have it at any price.

I said we'd feel bad to suggest 100 yuan because I knew it should cost more than that so we'd better not buy it at all. He asked for 150 and I told him no. But then, what the hell, okay. They just wear you down. 150.

Chen bid us goodbye with a spring in his step and a quarter of his monthly pay stuck down his pants, not so far from being an "individual businessman" himself, and we left with original Guilin art for twenty bucks.

•••••

Long was, as ever, full of tight-lipped cheer. It was her job. After she got us checked in for our flight to Shanghai and helped us pay the 50 yuan departure tax we tipped her and quickly it was Long, gone.

Third world architects determine the amount of light needed for a space, then halve it. Yellow lights in the ceiling solved nothing. Incense burned in the toilet. Noodles were eaten. A big red banner hung across the hall. The screen showed flights to Beijing, Guangzhou, Hong Kong, Shanghai, Chongqing and Xiamen.

In the drab domestic departures terminal, you wore your coat. There were gates 1, 2 and 3. No matter which gate you went through you'd come out at the same place on the other side and walk to your plane.

Our plane rolled down the runway and into the air 15 minutes early. Like good Communists striving for order, they seated passengers from the front straight back. That left the last two-thirds of the plane empty.

Before you knew it you could see how dark rural China was at night. Later the moon painted white the clouds below. The whole flight, not a word from the cockpit. We slumped down into our bright red (what else?) seats.

They apparently had Chinese people believing all the in-flight service they needed was some box of orange drink. But Mirja was in no mood for that and boldly asked for two cans of Shanghai Beer, and they brought them right out.

●●●●●

9 SRI LANKA

There are certain things a guidebook ought to level with you about right up front, before gushing about the exotic culture, pristine sandy beaches and friendly people. Number one, page one, straight flat out:

YOU ARE FLYING INTO A COUNTRY THAT CAN'T KEEP THE ROAD TO ITS ONE INTERNATIONAL AIRPORT PAVED, AND LINES THE ROAD IN AND OUT WITH BOYS WITH NO FACIAL HAIR HOLDING MACHINE GUNS.

Lurching into and out of potholes on the road from the airport to the beach, dim yellow headlights illuminated scrawny street dogs sneering from the road, teeth in road kill. Mirja and I took the diplomatic approach and decided, let's see what it looks like in the morning.

•••••

The fishing fleet already trolled off the Negombo shore in the gray before dawn. The last tardy catamaran, sail full-billowed, flew out to join the rest.

Sheldon had already been out and back. A slight fellow, just chest high, with a broad smile under a tight-clipped mustache, Sheldon showed me his catch, in a crate, a few gross of five or six inch mackerels.

He took me to meet all the other guys and see their catches, too, stepping over nets they were busy untangling and setting right for the afternoon. He led me to his house, just alongside and between a couple of beach hotels, shoreside from the road, among a sprawl of a dozen thatch huts.

Sheldon built it himself. It was before the 2004 Boxing Day tsunami and I don't know if it, or Sheldon and his family, are there anymore. He took me inside, immensely proud, to show me how he had arranged two hundred woven palm-frond panels on top of one another to build the roof. He told me "two hundred" over and over.

A thatch wall divided Sheldon's house into two rooms. The only furniture was a rough wooden bed with no linens.

Sheldon's wife, a very young woman dressed in a long blue and white smock with her hair pulled back, rose with a smile to greet me, and their precocious four and six year old daughters danced around us all. Sheldon took his son, just one year old, into his lap as we talked.

Sheldon and his family, Negombo Beach.

We sat together near a crack in the wall where sunlight came through so they could look at postcards of where I was from. They served sweet tea. I drank it fearing I'd pay for drinking the water later that day.

Sheldon walked me back toward Hotel Royal Oceanic, two hundred meters and several worlds apart. On the way, he explained to me that he was 31, his brother was "41, 42 sometimes. Lives nearby, Mama too. Papa no."

•••••

I'd plotted a Sri Lanka itinerary twice too ambitious. The roads were fine, really. There were just too many people trying to use them. The two lanes couldn't cope with the mass of people and machines vying for them.

If you weren't on a highway, or were at a sharp bend in one, you'd have to stop to let bigger vehicles squeeze by. And since there were no bypass roads for heavy trucks, and since most folks didn't have private cars but instead rode big, fat inter-city buses, you were forever stopping and starting and squeezing between milk trucks and cement mixers and buses, and in Sri Lanka there were also tuk-tuks, those three-wheeled two stroke vehicles used from Bombay to Bangkok to Borneo.

So we stopped for every bus. Our driver Tyrone joked about having to stop for women drivers, too. Our air conditioner "work very good, sir." That was a damn good thing on the coastal plain where, as we passed a cricket match at 10:15 in the morning, I thought them all positively fools, running around in long pants.

•••••

Provincial elections were to be held the next day. Election posters covered the buildings. Tyrone claimed 99% literacy in Sri Lanka (other sources suggest 90 per cent), but even so they used a system like in the much less literate Nepal. Each party was represented by a symbol, so that the illiterate could recognize their party and vote, in this case, for "chair" or "elephant" or "table" or "bell."

The main parties were the ruling Sri Lanka Freedom Party, in power for the last five years and advertised by posters of the president, Chandrika Kumaratunga, holding her hand high in the air, and the opposition United National Party, which had held power the prior seventeen years.

Plastic flags flew over the road like over a used car lot. Blue marked the incumbent party's territory, green the challengers'. By the plastic flag test, it would be the Freedom Party in a romp.

In a tradition of pre-election violence, a couple of weeks ago a woman blew herself up in Colombo. And a few years ago, days before a visit by Prince Charles, eight were killed near the Buddha's tooth shrine in Kandy, the second city and seat of power under the ancient kings.

Tyrone offered that, "I will be gathering information," about potential trouble. This morning's news was that a candidate in the east had been shot overnight. Yesterday was the last day of electioneering, with no rallies allowed from then.

That kind of violence baffled him, Tyrone said, and anyway it doesn't matter which party rules - they both promise the world until elected and then they don't do anything.

Some things are the same the world over.

He was puzzled why people took it all so seriously, he told us, when the leaders themselves don't; At the end of the day, he said, they sit down and "they have a drink together."

•••••

The wealthier houses presented whitewashed concrete walls to the road. Those funny-looking pointy-nosed one-cylinder "rototiller" tractors like they use in China were here, too.

Coconut plantations dominated the road to the main Colombo-Kandy highway. Bicycle carts pedaled by, some with wooden baskets built on back and scales cradled inside. Rolling, mobile merchants. Tyrone showed us a motorcycle with a box of little fish and said the guy goes door to door. Banana trees along the road, underneath tall coconut palms.

Everything grew here, I guessed. Mangoes were in season now, and avocados. Durians were out of season but they grew here, too. Tyrone called them the fruit that tastes like heaven but smells like hell.

Tyrone had fifteen years in the business and looked for all the world like a wiry, Sri Lankan Jeff Goldblum. He was good. He wasn't a young, adventurous boy-driver. He was comfortable in himself. He told us not too many Americans came here and we could see that.

Germans, Italians, Japanese and British came, but really it was mostly the Germans, with their big charter airline LTU discharging a crew at the hotel as we left, and copies of Bild, Bild Frau magazines and cheap German novels and crossword books lying around the lobby coffee tables.

•••••

We got the Kandy road and suddenly Tyrone got politics. He liked the Freedom party because they were pro-privatization. They one hundred percent privatized the tea plantations, for example. He couldn't cite a lot of other differences except the opposition was more socialist.

He guided us through a tangled story of ruling families and power politics that left me way behind. Sometimes he lapsed into tour-guidism ("Excluding inland waters, area of Sri Lanka is 65,000 square kilometers.").

The Kandy road was wide enough for two cars to pass side by side. As we began to bite off a little elevation en route to Kegalle, Tyrone returned to the matter of the elections. There would be a curfew, he thought, tomorrow night as the election results came in, and it would most likely last for 24 hours.

That suggested possible violence, I thought, but it seemed normal to Tyrone, and it came with a benefit. We could get a "special travel permit," and with the road less busy, "we can go ninety hundred," he laughed.

Kegalle was stifling hot and gridlocked with buses and tuk-tuks in both directions. Traffic police stood surrounded by the chaos and did no good that I could tell. It reminded me of the garrison town of Wangdi Phodrang in Bhutan, about which Barbara Crossette wrote, "welcoming, but exceptionally unappealing."

Four kilometers past Kegalle stood a road sign: "A home for domesticated, disabled and elderly elephants." We swung left into the elephant orphanage at Pinnawala.

All these elephants had become separated from their families in the national parks or in the wild; Maybe their families were shot for their tusks, for example. One had his right front foot blown off by a land mine.

The Pinnawala elephant orphanage.

Each elephant had his own individual trainer (there being no shortage of labor) and the trainers worked with their elephants all their lives. Asian elephants are trainable (we rode elephants in Nepal who would pick up logs, even trash, on their mahout's command), but that doesn't mean a trainer isn't occasionally killed, especially during mating season.

You could get in quite close and mingle with the elephants. Kids petted a little one. It was humane that they cared for the elephants but, scruffy and indolent as all of the herd was, the whole scene was a little downbeat.

•••••

Seamlessly, spice country turned to tea country. Looking around, you could believe that Sri Lanka supplied the whole world. Boys played cricket in the road and they had to, because there were tea bushes utterly everywhere else.

Over the front seat, Tyrone was explaining how buffalo milk mixed with honey is the local equivalent of yogurt, when up came two signs, one explaining we'd achieved an elevation of 6187 feet, the other reading "Welcome to the Salubrious Climes of Nuwara Eliya."

Straight through the scramble, at the far side of town stood the old British Grand Hotel. Nuwara Eliya (pronounced "Noo-relia") is an old British hill station, full of well-tended proper English gardens and lingering British-built structures like the Grand Hotel – dark, wooden, rambling, musty and old.

It's said that the Sinhalese preceded the Tamils to Ceylon and when the British arrived, the Sinhalese were unwilling to work for the slave wages the Brits wanted to pay. So the Brits recruited the Tamils and brought them up here to pick tea.

The good Tamils, as Tyrone called them, (not the trouble-causing Tamils agitating for independence) got housing, a stipend, a garden and a quota. After reaching quota they got a premium for the tea they picked, per kilo.

•••••

Six o'clock on election morning. Two loudspeakers chanted the call to Allah alongside a glass-enclosed Buddha statue just by the traffic circle. The sun hadn't cleared the hills but it was set to be a glorious morning, with birds and dew run riot.

At this hour, Nuwara Eliya served mostly as a staging area for the bus station. People queued and a few stores lumbered open. At a milk bar (that's a name they use for convenience stores from here to New Zealand) I bought toothpaste and remarked how it would be a nice day.

Dazzling smile: "It is election day, sir!"

•••••

Voters walked to polling stations. They got time off to vote, though voting wasn't mandatory.

We wouldn't find out about a prospective curfew until later, but Tyrone said all the drivers thought (they all stayed at a drivers' compound next to the hotel, like they do on East African package trips) that when the announcement was made, they'd all go down to the police station in the Nuwara Eliya town center and get travel permits.

•••••

During a beer at the St. Andrews Inn (where there was no sign of guests), afternoon clouds closed over hills that had just been gleaming in the sun, and before you knew it mist creeped into Nuwara Eliya.

Walking back the length of town, we stopped and shopped for a mango and some tiny peanuts. Mirja decided they're far better than the big ones back home, the way Roma tomatoes are tastier than the big round ones. The guy fashioned a bag from a folded sheet of newspaper. He scooped it full for thirty rupees.

A beaming boy, sleeves rolled up to his forearms, stood before a videotape and chocolate store chopping garlic and spring onions on an ancient stovetop. It smelled delicious.

This was a real vacation day, way out on a trip, not coming or going, no travel, no agenda, no problem. We fired up the heater in mid-afternoon. I turned on the shortwave, as just now was NATO's thirteenth night of bombing Serbia. In 1999, the internet hadn't quite yet supplanted the shortwave.

Grilling lunch in Nuwara Eliya.

•••••

Chair won. The ruling alliance represented by the chair symbol gained ground, although they lost seats in Colombo and its suburbs. Tyrone told us the results but I knew them because I saw an animated chair doing a little jig on morning TV. Later, the BBC World Service called it a muddle, no clear victor, no mandate for either side.

There was some violence in Matale, north of Kandy, but the curfew the drivers had expected was only from eleven last night to five a.m. Still, at a police checkpoint at the edge of Nuwara Eliya town, the cop wanted us to go way around the other way, but Tyrone lied that he didn't know that way.

The vote: People's Alliance 2,105,546, United National Party 1,979,546, making up 70 per cent of registered voters. "No deaths have been reported.... The majority of the complaints were of a minor nature, bordering on threats, abuse and cases of simple hurt...." as the paper put it.

•••••

Tyrone didn't do bags. He'd call a bell boy. He'd let Mirja and me haul them. He wouldn't touch 'em. He'd spend fifteen minutes guarding them in the lobby instead of loading them up.

But what a gorgeous day! Tyrone in his British driving cap, the air crisp and fresh, we set off at 7:30 sharp, down from the highlands, and we drove five and a half hours to get 160 kilometers. Five and a half hours for 100 miles.

Mist filtered the sunlight way up in the hills outside Nuwara Eliya as we drove past orchids grown for export around Lake Gregory, alongside the old British horse racing track on the east side of town, and then down toward Bandarawela.

•••••

Mirja had a cold, started a week before. What better way to chase it than an herbal massage at the renowned Suwa Madhu Indigenous, Eight-fold Ayurvedic Treatment and Manufacturers of Herbal Medicine and Beauty Cream Institute of Sri Lanka, just on the far side of Bandarawela town?

Seemed to do the trick. She came out hair up, oily and grinning.

While the institute did its magic, I wandered down the street to a communal spring and watched babies being washed by laughing kids, scarcely older, everybody splashing and playing in the pool. The oldest girl invited me home for tea. They placed a tiny cup in my lap and the whole family of eight watched me drink from it. I showed them postcards of home and they showed me their pride and joy, the oldest boy, away at the police academy, as photographed in his class picture.

Green double doors with a tassel of string instead of a door knob led to an anteroom that may have begun as the color of peach, but the plaster had long ago cracked and smudged. Three framed photos, all askance, decorated the otherwise bare walls as mama, graying at the temples, in sandals and a print skirt, sat in a high, straight-backed chair with her hands clasped in her lap, smiling, surrounded by her brood.

The youngest, a precious brown-eyed beauty, took shy refuge behind an intricately hand-carved chair, only her head and hands visible. I may have been a stranger, but she offered a ready, open smile.

Big smile, safe behind the chair.

Rolling across the flats bound for the coast, buildings, painted all over, advertised Sunlight, Astra, Vim, Signal, Rinso and Lifebuoy household products, and "Curd & Hunny."

In monastery towns monks climbed on and off the buses. There were branches of Peoples Bank - "The Bank with a Heart" - and here was Triple Star Services - "A New Meaning to Cleaning." Once we found ourselves trapped for a while by the Chirpy Chip truck - "From the House of Uswatte."

Bikes hauling bananas plied the roadway, now alongside cactus and sawgrass. Marsh and wetland, salt pans, lagoons and windmills covered the Sri Lankan south.

We beat a tour bus into the otherwise empty Oasis Hotel at a place called Hambantota, where they played bad disco at lunch, and the waiters tried proper, formal serving techniques, barefoot. They smiled sweet as the day is long, but couldn't pour a non-foamy Carlsberg.

Walking into the lobby, Tyrone gleamed, "How do you like it?" We turned to look around and he said, "My father was project manager for this entire complex. But he died before grand opening." We told him we liked it real well.

At 2:45 two guys named Nandiga and Chaminda showed up in what had formerly passed for a jeep, and away we went to look for elephants.

Nandiga smoked cigarettes like the French do in movies, forefinger and thumb, as he hurtled back across roads we'd crossed much more carefully earlier in the day. At the park entrance, Chaminda moved from the front seat to stand upon the back benches, the canvas top now off.

We bumped along adjacent to the shore, sometimes coming right upon it, for maybe three hours and saw more elephants than you'd think, maybe six or seven, but all of them looked cornered by the inevitable convergence of several jeeps - except for a female and male our jeep found first. We gave them distance as they watered themselves, courted, nuzzled and played.

We saw iguanas and monkeys, but it was really all about birds - over 20,000 in the park at any given time, they say. So we saw migratory wild ducks from Siberia, and sandpipers, jungle fowl, peacocks, peahens, gulls, plovers, terns, a few green parrots, egrets, pelicans, herons and storks. And a crocodile. Chaminda knew where to look.

Nandiga knew the park, too. At 22, he'd been working here nine years, as a helper before he got his drivers license, since then as a safari master. He drove like 23 year olds do the world over, but we made it home. Hey, it wasn't Africa but it was fun, and hey, this safari only cost $26.50.

•••••

"When does the monsoon come?" I asked Tyrone.

"End of April, sir."

"Is it ever late?"

"It is always late, sir."

•••••

The sun was out at first in the morning, but by mid-morning, a soft, silver cast covered the sky, and storm clouds scudded up in the west. Surf crashed against shore, so tall that there were no stilt fishermen at Talpe. Their stilts swayed naked in the surf.

We passed a truck labeled on each side, simply, "Retort."

•••••

Matara, just by the lighthouse at Dondra Head, had a seething bus terminal, where people jumped on and off buses while they were still rolling. There was a massive tuk-tuk parking lot and a central market, and even one or two modern glass buildings. With all that, still, at the southern tip of Ceylon, bullock carts ruled.

•••••

At Galle, at the ramparts of the Portugese fort (finished by the Dutch) streets were still Dutch-named. Every town along the coast was just like the last, hardscrabble, vendors selling only the things you need to live, no luxury. People, bicycles, buses, tuk-tuks, bullock carts and us - all sharing the lane and a half of blacktop.

Famous mask factories make special masks for exorcisms at the town of Ambalangoda. If you're Catholic they're exorcisms. If not, it's chasing out evil spirits or chasing off the evil eye. At the Ambalangoda mask museum ancient legends and fairy tales are explained, and you can see masks of each of the eighteen Sanni Demons.

"These demons are very powerful and dangerous. They can make people sick by looking at them."

There they all were, one by one, causing diseases of the bile, stomach pain, measles, mumps, diarrhea, poison like cobra poison in the body, and blister. And there was Gedi Sanniya, who causes furuncles.

Ambalangoda mask factory.

Spice garden number 100 ("private but approved by the tourist board"), provided a complete regime of 22 remedies, with explanations, just like in Guilin, including, for example #3 cinnamon oil against tooth pain: "Put a drop into the cavity of the tooth, when saliva acumulates spite it out again put one drop into the cavity repeat four times." Or #13 kamayogi bon-bon: "Indicated in pre-ejaculation, the 1/2 teaspoon ful paste of kamayogi bon-bon eat before sexual affinity to control the pre-ejaculation and other debilities. Better before twenty minutes the sex and have some milk more."

A train blocked the road in Bentota town, where there was a man whose all-day job was to stand there and close the gates for the five trains a day.

An elephant that was due to work in a wedding ceremony blocked the narrow little road to the beach for a time, but by mid-afternoon we inhabited a beachfront bungalow at Kasgoda beach. The surf crashed hard forty meters away. I rented a fridge for $3 a day and six Heinekens were in there cooling.

Chipmunks, cows and coconut palms on shore. Southbound geese offshore. A day at the beach. I'd gotten into a little Glenfiddich the night before and woke slow, had a Thai chilli-laced omelet and retired to the porch to read *The Teaching of Buddha*, supplied along with the New Testament in French, English and German.

The sea sounded a dull roar, and palm fronds caused a wind-whipped tempest, but offshore blue sky peeked through here and there. Occasionally a manic low black cloud raked the manicured lawn with water-fire. We put on the Sri Lanka music channel and Mirja did a long walk and found a turtle hatchery down the beach, and lots of eager-to-be-your-friend Sri Lankans.

A chipmunk climbed down the palm tree beside the porch and stared at me from three feet away. The wind blew things around inside our room. I felt bad for the people who'd come to lie in the sun, but I loved it. The earth was vividly, furiously alive.

How many Sri Lankans did it take to change a lightbulb? In our case three, several trips to the shop and about thirty minutes. They had to change the whole fixture.

●●●●●

10 MADAGASCAR

Weeks-long rains had very nearly drowned the capital of Madagascar. Water filled the fields around Antananarivo, locally known as Tana, and giant sea birds crowded Lake Anosy.

At the airport, Mr. Andriamanohy Rantoanison, Manou, showed us a laminated card with the prix fixée: 44000 FMG.

It was essential to speak some French here, and Manou the Malagasy (pronounce that "Malagash") Francophone, Mirja and I did it well together, less from skill than from good will, patience and good humor.

Manou brought us to the Mad Hilton, where they served raisin juice for a welcome drink. You see the same picture of Tana in all of the few guidebooks. Now we saw it too. Your intrepid backpacking-guide author stayed at the Hilton.

Antananarivo, Madagascar.

Tana sprawled across several hilltops and the Hilton was set back from the town opposite Lake Anosy. In the middle of the lake stood a monument in commemoration of Le Première Guerre Mondiale, and along the shore floated leaves that couldn't have been more green. They fairly glowed. Glew?

The sun dropped behind clouds before sunset. New in town, we stayed in our room a few floors up, attacked the minibar and warily eyed the busy, dusking-up streets around the lake.

The Malagasy are not brewers. I spat out a Madagascar-brewed Golden-something. Spat it out. Golden left a wicked curl in your tongue and a sour aftertaste.

•••••

Zoma means Friday and it's also the name for the positively teeming Friday market in Tana.

It's strange to prepare for theft, but that's what they admonish. Fix your bag to minimize what they get if they slash it open. *The Bradt Guide to Madagascar*: "The Zoma is notorious for thieves. It is safest to bring only a small amount of money in a money belt or neck pouch. Enticingly bulging pockets will be slashed."

From a hill above Independence Avenue, a sea of white umbrellas washed out ahead in every direction, swallowing up the main square, flowing into busy little eddies beside stairways, up the hills as far as the eyes could see. Up one hill, down the next.

We paused. This was big, sprawling, daunting and dramatic. We clasped hands and dove in. Flowers first, down on the right. Then a jumble of sundries, the multitudes and the advertised danger, rarefied by the dry hot sun.

Someone reached out and tugged at Mirja's skirt. Beware the "voleurs," she warned.

Buy whatever you will. Locks and hinges. Grenadine drinks. Bright plastic jugs. Chicago Bulls caps. Greasy food rolls. Major motor parts. Michael Jackson T-shirts. A vast selection of wicker. Bon Bon Anglais Limonad. We bought a "Madagascar" ink-pad stamp that actually printed "Madagascap."

Must've been three or four hundred meters down one side. Too tight to turn, too close to walk two abreast, too tense to relax. Still, smiles from the stalls. Dignity, not desperation. Smiles, and lots of open looks of wonder.

All the way down and halfway back we didn't spy anyone from our part of the world, probably for an hour.

Baby clothes. The tiniest shoes you've ever seen. Embroidery. Crocheting - napkins and table covers embroidered with lemurs and scenes from traditional life.

The Malagasy are a little smaller than me in general and I was forever bumping my head on the edges of their big white umbrellas, knocking my sunglasses off my head.

Mirja tried on mesh vests.

Down by the train station, the varnished wooden trunk section. Turning back, furniture. Circuit boards. Tiny piles of tacks. Stacks of feed bags.

There is a classic trap: there is a Malagasy 5000 Franc note. Then there is another that says 5000 also in numbers, but instead of reading merely "arivo ariary," it reads "dimy arivo ariary," which I believe means five times five thousand and in any event definitely means 25000 Malagasy Francs, even though in numbers it says 5000.

The feed bag guy wanted 1100 (27.5 cents) for a multicolored "Madagascar" bag. Realizing it just as the bill left my hand, I gave him not a proper 5000 but one of the 5000's that are really 25000. After a lot of consultation with a lot of people, I got the correct 23900 in change.

We walked up each side of the Zoma - past the train station, bureaux travel, the Library of Madagascar, and made it to the top of an adjoining hill unrobbed.

Here at the top of the hill stood the country's symbols of power: the Central Bank, High Court, Ministry du Promotion de l'Industry. A band was set up to play on a flatbed but never did. There was hubbub, amplified music and lots and lots of people. Up here the kid beggars that you usually tolerate because objectively, their circumstance ain't like yours, swarmed so that they might have carried us away, so we turned aggressive and swatted 'em back.

Crowd at the Zoma, Tana.

By midday, unscathed and self-satisfied, we sat with our backs to the wall like in any good western, at the Hotel Colbert's terrace bar, already having seen a week's worth in one morning. Hotel Colbert had a dubious five star rating, apparently not from any organization in particular.

It was a gorgeous day and the city was so picturesque, completely foreign. We ordered Heinekens in the haze. At Hotel Colbert smoking was still as big as it ever was. Yellow Benson and Hedges ashtrays as big as your head took up a quarter of each table, and flaccid, bibulous Frenchmen sat nursing their Three Horses Beers, and hacked and smoked too much.

Four ceiling fans, all whipping. Glass tabletops. No magasin (store) at this five star. The clerk unkindly suggested I go out to scrap with the local boys to find a newspaper. I wasn't successful, or grateful.

•••••

One night, at a restaurant across town, we sat working our way through the national dish, romazava, a meat and vegetable stew with ginger on the side containing "brèdes," which is pronounced "bread" and is in fact greens.

The lights dimmed for the floor show, an unself-conscious, barefoot, foot-stompin' celebration - white teeth behind brown faces. Boys pranced in costumes of yellow feed sacks and chubby girls all whirled and sang at the tops of their lungs.

Another night we watched a surging mob, malevolent like snakes writhing in a bag. Hoping it was the start of a coup maybe (Madagascar is good for a coup every five or six years), we rushed up to the second floor to see better. Probably 30 or 40 young toughs ran down the rue.

There in the dusk, in front of a big window in a Hilton conference room with no lights on, we quizzed a young security man.

His reply, "They are fighting," perfectly illuminated everything. In the end it turned out to be just some pedestrian rivalry among kids from the Lycée Ampefiloha down the street.

•••••

The most recent journal en Anglais in the Madagascar Hilton was the Wall Street Journal Europe from the fifteenth, ten days before. Just as we sat down to catch up on the news, Manou came driving up the ramp at 7:00 sharp, right on time.

Manou might have been a smidge younger than I first thought. He had English well worse than our combined rudimentary French, but we conveyed some really abstract ideas both ways in the course of the day - alongside the inevitable, "We eat corn. Do you?" "Yes yes! we eat corn too!!" type of linguistic breakthroughs.

Manou had two daughters, 15 and 13. He was trim and fit, with salt and pepper hair of the Merina, the interior people. The coastal people are descended from Africans and have coarser hair. The Merina, including Manou, are fairer, almost olive-skinned, and said to be of Indonesian origin.

Manou's eyes were expressive, crinkly. His only trip off the island was about as likely as a family of four from Des Moines vacationing in Macau: Once Manou had a patron who took him to be a croupier in Djibouti.

•••••

Our plan was to travel south down the spine of Madagascar just west of a line of hills called the Ankaratra range 160 kilometers, to the town of Antsirabe (Malagasy town names sound vaguely Sri Lankan, long, flouncy words full of both consonants and vowels, like the towns in Sri Lanka called Warakapola and Ambalangoda and Batticaloa). Antsirabe is home to hot springs and a hotel, and reasonably accessible via the improved road, Autoroute Nationale Numéro Sept, the N 7. There's a lot you read about Madagascar that's not true, but they were right when they wrote that the N7 highway is flat and smooth.

Everything began spectacularly - cool in the highlands, with sun and cumulus and very blue skies. As we sped in and right back out of the first town, Tranombarotra, we established our communication ground rules: Speak slowly, and keep trying.

Manou wondered about the predictable driver's concerns: What do we drive in the U.S.? How much is it? How much is gas?

He spent a little more time looking back at us than I might have preferred. Finally though, as he began a poorly understood synopsis of Malagasy politics, Manou turned back to regard the highway. First Republic, with the French, was "fantastic." Second Republic, starting in '73, "no good." Friends like Libye, Irak and Corée du Nord.

Manou had a special hate for the North Koreans, who would fly in and demand rides to the president's palace and not pay, an unhappy reality enforced by the presidential guard. The North Koreans built the palace for President Didier Ratsiraka on the other side of some hills south of Tana.

Manou stopped for us to take pictures of it (which would have been at our peril in the old days) framed in the foreground by mud-hut squalor. Massive and multi-level. Ratsiraka tried to be king, said Manou.

Didier Ratsiraka's palace.

The Malagasy abhor conflict. Some 400,000 people organized and marched down here from Tana in August,

1991. Ratsiraka put machine gunners in the hills and lobbed grenades into the marchers, killing a hundred or so (the government said eleven). Even thus outraged, it took the consensus-building Malagasy another two years to oust the guy in elections, as, no fool he, Ratsiraka overnight became the world's best capitalist and most sincere promiser.

Ratsiraka had shot up his own people. But the Berlin wall had fallen and so had his income from the Soviets. He presented himself as a candidate in elections, lost but officially won, and finally lost for real. Now he lives in France.

One of the things you'll read about Madagascar that's just not true is that all the hills are clear cut and stripped, denuded down to the red earth. The hills are mostly bare, but they're green, rather like Hawaii in lushness, and rather like Scotland for the tree-free, rolling moor feel. Most of the land is under cultivation, terraced for rice, but with some corn and a little blé (wheat).

Boulders were strewn across fields and rounded hills for the first 45 kilometers south of Tana. Not breathtaking. Oddly pretty. Everybody, man, woman and child, wore a straw hat. The houses were long and lanky and thin, a peculiar tall style, concrete or brick, sunbaked red either way, most often thatch roofed but sometimes tin.

In Vietnam, the colonial French taxed houses based on their width, resulting in tall, thin buildings. These were like that.

Another thing you'll read is how powerful is the animist belief system of taboos, or fadys. Now here was a tiny village of twelve or 15 red houses - and the two tallest buildings were Christian churches - the Protestant, then the Catholic.

Roads like the N 7 hold motorized traffic, of course, but with not so many cars, these roads are also used for walking. Since pedestrians share the road with cars, you're forever having nerve-rattling near misses, as cars won't slow down and walkers don't jump to the shoulder until the very last second.

Add pollution, the need to constantly pass broken down trucks, tiny kids, occasional zebus (a type of cattle), and constant horns, and you've got life on the N 7. A thigh-high clump of weeds in your lane serves as a notice that there's someone broken down beyond a curve ahead, usually with two or four bare legs underneath the vehicle, extending still further into the road.

The road had been curvy down to Ambatolampy, about halfway to Antsirabe. Zebu carts far outnumbered cars and refreshingly, there were almost no motorbikes or mopeds. At Ambatolampy, Manou knew of an American with a Malagasy wife who ran a horse stable. Did we want to stop?

So just on the other side of town we turned up a dirt track at a sign, "Manja Ranch 1 km." and spoke English with the man of the house. He'd just awakened (it wasn't yet 9:00), didn't offer his name, and drank tea without offering us any. Just another anti-establishmentarian who couldn't or didn't want to do it the American way - from St. Louis, posted here as an engineer eight years ago.

Quit, married locally, stayed. Goatee, a little wild-eyed intensity, and a 70's-mod orange and blue striped shirt. He'd started the horse farm, with a half dozen or so horses and more servants, and he was trying to entice groups from Tana down into the hills.

First, he needed to get into the guidebooks, of which there were then exactly two: Hilary Bradt's Guide to Madagascar ("I don't know why we're not in there." He felt it personally. "We've written her. People have written her for us. But you know, she's getting lazy. She only comes to Madagascar three weeks a year anymore.") and the Lonely Planet guide, in which he'd got a mention ("They stole a lot of stuff from Hilary.").

He groused that the government counted every arrival as a tourist arrival and thus while there were 52,000 "tourists" last year, really there were only about 30 or 35,000. The government kept ticket prices too high, there was no reason this country should be as poor as it was.

He blamed Ratsiraka but also his predecessors for taking too long to jump start tourism. This would be the year that decided whether they would stay or sell and go. He muttered quite a bit.

It was a couple hundred meters higher than even the king's and queen's hilltop palaces in Tana out here, and when clouds covered the sun it got positively chilly. We bumped and rolled on back down toward Ambatolampy.

Manou said rice cost 2000 Mfr per kilo, or 50 cents for 2.2 pounds, and that was an outrageously high price he thought, given all the rice in all the fields.

When he'd ask something in French, we'd decipher and try to answer and he'd always reply with an endearing, "Aaahhhhhhhh!," the secrets of the universe being revealed, when really we told him things like the English word for vache is cow.

After Ambatolampy the N 7 straightened out and we really cruised. The town before Antsirabe, Ampitatafika, marked a transition. The landscape flattened and the crops changed from terraced rice paddies to fields of maize. From here on in, people squatted at the roadside over covered iron pots on wood fires - steaming ears of corn for sale.

We traced along a muddy brown river through little villages, all red brick, with the rail line to our left. We stopped on a bluff 27 kilometers out of Antsirabe and did a roll of film (we took rolls of film in the 1990s) of the kids in the fields far below. Manou asked about U.S. racial problems and confided Madagascar's, between the highland Merina and coastal peoples - even though we're all brown, he smiled.

We drove right into and straight out of Antsirabe, straight on to Lac Andraikiba, a beautiful clean deep blue bowl free from crowds except for kids. We shook off the few kids begging for stylos and took a 30 minute stroll along the bank. Three or four girls washing clothes giggled. A canoe with two men paddled silently toward the center of the lake.

Rowing on Lac Andraikiba.

A man with a basket on his head tried to sell me something to either eat, chew or smoke. Whatever it was I told him "non, merci," and we walked back.

Screaming bright blue and red tiny flowers. Eucalyptus trees. The path thick with grasshoppers. They "thp-thp-thpped" by.

Manou dropped us for Heinekens at the Hotel des Thermes in Antsirabe, which is this mad colonial pink and white bemehoth hulk. It ain't pretty but it did have cold beer.

That's important because the Star brewery is right here in town and when it comes to Malagasy superlatives there is only one: the worst alcohol award. Golden Beer is just pucker-up-and-spit awful. Three Horses is likewise pucker-up awful and it was awarded the Monde Medal d'Or at Bruxelles in 1992, which unquestionably undermines that award forevermore.

But here were Heinekens - and brown Malagasy kids swimming in the pool, and a gaggle of Scandinavians, all mixed with a Japanese bus tour. Mirja had Malagasy wine, "vin gris," or gray wine - Gris de Manamisoa, from Ambalavao and it tasted about as good as its name.

But this was truly a beautiful, gorgeous day. Unusual evergreens and billowing white, clean clouds.

Then it was time for the pousse-pousse ride. As far as I can tell, Antsirabe is pretty clearly the pousse-pousse capital of the world. A pousse-pousse is a cyclo without the pedals - literally a push-push - because the driver is inside a little wood frame with a bar, attached to the seat over 16 inch wheels, and he has to push-push the bar to move. It's a Malagasy rickshaw.

They were absolutely everywhere, hand painted, individually named carriages named after girlfriends, movies, towns, rock stars. So we sat with a tiny old man pulling us along, bare feet slapping the pavement, getting going faster down hills, laboring up the other sides. Up the road to the Antsirabe train station, then a turn and a promenade down the grand avenue to the Hotel des Thermes and back. 2000 plus a 500 tip was 60 cents and he was delighted.

It's hard to imagine the life of a guy who can't afford shoes but still has to haul a cart full of people around on pavement - then it starts to rain and he has to just keep on hauling.

The pousse-pousses of Antsirabe.

Women washed clothes in a canal down by the thermal bathhouse you can't use anymore, and laid them on the ground to dry.

Blue gray clouds scudded in, kicked up a breeze and dumped a little rain on Antsirabe as we stopped at the Hotel Diamand restaurant. The stable man back in Ambatolampy told us it was the only place in town to eat, believe him, so we asked Manou to drive us by for lunch before heading out.

On the plus side it had a color TV and a bar, "Nightclub Tahiti." The most expensive thing on the menu was Camembert cheese at $5 a kilo. Crab meat was not quite $2. Hygiene was the only factor on the other side of the ledger, and it was enough to keep us from eating.

Manou, though, could as good as taste the zebu as we left Antsirabe, I guess, because he laid on the gas and got us back to Tana in just over two and a half hours, compared to something like four hours on the way down. And at these prices, ol' Manou and Madame Manou would be wadin' in zebu for weeks.

I'm not sure what makes a zebu, really. How or if it's different from a steer. But one man's bullock is another man's zebu, I always say.

Grapes, corn and green apples, offered for sale on the roadside. Blé in the fields.

Manou was probably a pretty good businessman. Didn't much claim to like his Peugeot 504, but he still had it souped up with Pioneer woofers and tweeters cut into the back.

We were just rollin' along at the 39 kilometer marker outside Tana when BAM!!!!!!

Glass splintered, we swerved and Mirja and I jerked awake. I whirled to see a cock flying into the grass behind us.

We stopped. The left headlight was busted away.

Already a man was approaching the cock in the high grass. We had our second glass-breaking ride, after Burma, Manou had a repair bill and somebody had an unexpected dinner behind us.

Soon enough the scramble of stalls, like "Poissonerie," down at the paddies signaled the edge of Tana. Twenty-plus year old metallic Renaults. Tatas, polluting as usual. But to be fair, in Madagascar, so did all the other buses - Mitsubishis, Mercedes and Izusus, too.

•••••

They wouldn't buy back your local money when you left Madagascar. Since we had maybe $80 worth we were tipping fools that last day, ordering onion soup, bread with goat cheese, entrecôte with sauce, all we could eat at lunch, and being forced into Three Horses Beer, endured in the 65 centilitre size, because the Heinekens ran out.

We had evaded theft our entire stay, but we pressed our luck with one last trip to Avenue de l'Independence. Our luck ran out.

The idea was to spend a couple hundred thousand Francs. So we bought some art and a musical instrument we only mildly wanted, beat away the vending crowd and climbed into a taxi, where a kid reached in the window and pulled Mirja's gold bracelet right from her wrist. He bolted around the corner, into the crowd and away.

Damn.

••••••

11 TIBET

Ashray Raj Gautam waited in the dark before dawn. Men worked under the hood of his Toyota Corolla while we stuffed our things in its trunk. We pushed the car down the hill to get it started, and little Gautam took us to a town called Banepa, north of Kathmandu. Mirja bought junk food, I bought cheap Indian whiskey, and Gautam disappeared.

We waited for a long time, and when he came back, Gautam had a confession. He did a sheepish, dusty little shuffle.

"We came here with no fan belt."

He was sure we could get one in Banepa but he couldn't find one.

"Excuse me sir, we have to wait for new car from Kathmandu one hour." He went to find a phone.

So we were off, sort of, driving from Kathmandu to Lhasa. Our Tibet travel permits would be waiting at the border. The fellow who booked us said don't bring pictures of the Dalai Lama (I had five), and don't be surprised if the police follow you - they're not too used to private visitors.

Banepa, Nepal, was a lane and a half of bad tarmac twenty kilometers outside Kathmandu, with twenty meters of dust on either side of the road, and businesses the length of town with their garage-door-fronts rolled down closed.

Buses bumped into the dust and blasted their horns. They shared the verge with chickens, goats, kids, bags of grain, metal rods and tubes, the general refuse, and us.

Two old folks worked the length of town with rough straw brooms, whipping up a dust tornado, moving trash from here to there to no use. Boys held up bread into the windows of the buses. They spit and coughed all the time.

It's no surprise life expectancy is 55 in Nepal. In Banepa the air was opaque. You couldn't even see the neighborhood hills. Forget the Himalayas, you couldn't see out of town.

Banepa, Nepal.

Gautam borrowed 500 rupees for gas for the replacement Corolla. We needed oil, but we couldn't find any and drove on. A road sign declared: "Khodari - 85 km." The border.

For a long time we drove up one side or the other of the Botaghosi. Bo means Tibet, Bota means from Tibet and Ghosi means river. It ran green and chalky and it ran wild.

Cable for cablecars stretched across the river, shut down for years. People cut and stacked rocks. They dried homemade paper in the sun. Chalky dust covered everything.

Thirty kilometers from the border the tarmac dissolved into rocks. Clouds drew closer (rather we to them). Signs, "rock falling area." Now it was a meter by meter trudge. I was sure we'd break down but we bumped all the way into Khodari, sometimes along the river, sometimes on a track cut out of the hill.

We surrendered our passports. I had to pee. A cop motioned me around the side to pee on the Nepal checkpoint building.

Six hours, 88 kilometers. Flyin'.

Businessmen and thieves congregated on both sides of the border, and there were porters to pay to carry our bags over the bridge. We graduated from the Corolla to a LandCruiser, and headed into the border town on the Tibetan side called Zhangmu.

Our new staff: a driver, a "helper," our Chinese minder, a businessman in a suit to handle it all, and a bully in a tank top, earrings, ponytail and Nike cap - expediter.

Customs, Health declaration, Entry paper, Please come with me to restaurant, very clean. I get Tibet travel permit.

There were more flies in very clean Restaurant Gyan Glen than on our horse farm, but in the end it was two hours forty minutes of bureaucracy with no hassles. Good, courteous, smilin' folks.

•••••

Just above town, a roadblock. Show your papers, move on through. If the guard is Tibetan, who cares about your papers? Only the Chinese.

Watch for work crews. There would be a green-uniformed cadre sitting somewhere in the shade, supervising. They had to start their careers in a half-horse outpost like this, driving around miserable in an old red LandCruiser with a tiny red light on top. Made me smile.

•••••

Fifty kilometers to Nylam, riding up high in the LandCruiser, steady climbing. Where Nepal had huge pine forests, Tibet showed spruce and fir trees, with tiny new spring growth. I swore dogwoods and azaleas bloomed across the way.

Up the Botaghosi (must be named something else now), our first herd of Zoh - a mix of yak and bull - led to yaks, big humps behind their shoulders and long hair, and then the trees were just completely gone - not there. Rocky, barren. Snow appeared high up on the hilltops. On the far side of the Himalayas the sky turned cobalt blue.

•••••

A row of tin-roofed sheds on either side of the Lhasa road, Nylam was nothing more. Up a ladder across the street, a no-name restaurant served dinner of pork fat, green chillies and fries. We took diarrhea pills as prophylactics.

Two horse blankets sewn together hung over the front door of the Nylam Snow Land Hotel. Mirja sized up the situation quickly and immediately decided to go to sleep, the sooner to rise and leave.

The Snow Land was full. Our room was normally the proprietors', with a sandal under my bed. The girl who normally slept there slept on the bench behind the reception desk.

Late at night, someone convened an improbable meeting of evangelical Christians. You could hear them through the wall. They read from the Bible and I understood a woman with a Japanese accent giving testimony as I drifted off with a feeling I hadn't felt for thirty years - the warmth and safety of the sound of my parents in the next room talking softly after I had gone to bed.

I feared for lice and Mirja for vermin. Mirja saw the toilet once and never ventured there again. At first light we lined up beside the other guests to brush our teeth outside the front door and spit our bottled water into the street.

Mirja stood by the LandCruiser and said something as I carried bags into the street.

"What?" I asked.

"Don't step in the puke, I said," she said, too late.

The other foreigners, who stayed in proper rooms up on the Snow Land's upper floors, masked their unease with brusqueness. It was that kind of place.

The Snow Land Hotel.

They strapped our gear down and promised two hundred forty or fifty kilometers, nine hours and two passes over 5000 meters, and we set out alternately blazin' downhill then crawlin' too slow up hills, through wide valleys with thin streams of winding water. Just occasional scrubby brush, waist high tops. Way, way down to the bottom.

A truck sat mired in the middle of the track. We edged around it in rocks on the shoulder, just on the edge of God-knows-how-far down.

Giant rock fields. First came a village called Pamas, right on the river. What was the name of the river?

"No special name."

Our "helper" sort of – maybe - made us understand that this river and others come from the Nylam pass up ahead, so collectively they are all known as Nylam rivers.

We'd drive alongside walled, multi-family settlements built of stone with courtyards for livestock, which had their own way in and out. We'd pass a lone horseman, or three or four on a horse cart. I thought the sun might not make it into the valley until noon.

We didn't quite understand why we'd drive so slowly up the inclines. Mirja first suggested that maybe not gunning it was a way to not trigger landslides. Then, across rocky plains, she suggested more weakly, school zones? Turned out our driver didn't know "downshift."

Ponies led a cart filled with grain. One yak. A whitewashed stupa. Stone markers every kilometer. The first one I saw read 5380. To where?

First answer: Lhasa. Second try: the Tibet border. Truth: Beijing.

•••••

Hurtling (sometimes) across the Tibetan plateau. The Pakistani band Junoon on the juke, then some rasta tunes. "Stand up for your rights. Get up, stand up, don't give up the fight," our crew sang out loud and un-ironically.

•••••

We'd spy patches of snow. Way up high, over 14,000 feet, we felt light of breath. Mirja took her steroids and although her ears popped, she felt okay. I thought things started to move a little bit in slow motion. Everything was just very vivid, like in the seconds before a car crash.

Here was a landscape of stretched horizons. River beds with only a trickle of water wound through gorges half a mile wide or more. After a time we'd climbed so high that there were ice fields in whole mountains down below.

Prayer flags at the Lalung Leh Pass, 16570 feet.

We stood a little tight in the chest, temples pounding, at the prayer flags at the Lalung Leh pass at 5050 meters (16570 feet), and gazed on the peaks of Xixibangma, at 8012 meters, to the west, and Cho Oyu (8153) off to the east in the Qomolangma Nature Preserve. Qomolangma is the local name for Sagarmatha, or Everest, and Cho Oyu is the highest peak in the range west of Sagarmatha. Everest grew closer.

We had a little engine trouble, still in sight of the prayer flags. The LandCruiser was idling a little low and they had to climb up under the hood to prime the carburetor. While they did, Mirja and I clambered back out for more of the view, the cold, dry wind chapping our faces, and once the engine fired we moved on. Thrilled at the prospect of Everest ahead, we had no idea how much time would be spent under that hood.

By midday we were blazing across Tibet. The boys passed between them strings of yak cheese.

•••••

No more bushes - just patches of grass. You might have been watching everything through a wide angle lens.

A sheep herd, pushed by nomads, blocked the road. We jumped out of the LandCruiser into real, don't live anywhere nomads, maybe forty people in all, most under thirty, about a dozen of them children.

Everyone wore a sturdy, zippered coat and a head cover, an array of bright red patterned scarves and kerchiefs – on their heads, around their necks or under their hats. Two men carried crossbows and handmade fiddles on their backs.

Part of the swarm begged "money money money" but not belligerently, except when I tried to give two five yuan notes - a dollar twelve - to the man I imagined to be the headman. He snatched them from my hand before the little boys could.

The head nomads.

Every kid and his clothes were unwashed and nasty. Tiny girls carried even tinier infants on their backs. A small boy scowled from his perch tied to the back of a donkey.

•••••

High plateau Tibetan villages follow the same plan - the traditional whitewashed stone, with orange and blue vertical stripes painted from the roofs, and prayer flags rising from the four corners of the roofs. Though we'd dropped from the heights of the pass, we remained on the higher Tibetan plateau and patches of snow filled the folds of the hills.

Ruins of dzongs sat far up the hillsides. Dry, barren, rocky river beds stretched for miles. Just the barest grass grew and far off a cluster of shepherds grazed baby sheep, yaks and mules.

At a place called Gutso, green-uniformed sweepers tidied up the grounds of a hospital. A stark, tall white stupa stood at a bend. Om Mani Padme Hum in Tibetan script was carved into a barren hillside to salve the soul of the transitory Tibetan.

Mt. Everest from Tinggri village.

Beginning the traverse of a wide valley, we came face to face with Mt. Everest. Snow blew in waves off its peak. It was such a singular sight, Mirja and I piled out and sort of sat stupidly and stared for long moments, in silence and in awe.

Our boys finally urged us on. They reassured us that we could see Everest again at the village of Tinggri.

Turned out they sought Tinggri because that was where lunch was, at Amdo Guest House, ten rooms opening onto a courtyard. They were right, though, Everest was in full view from either end of the hundred-meter-long settlement. While they disappeared inside to eat, Mirja and I walked the town.

We traded caps with the kids, took pictures of pony riders and inspected sacks of tsampa, Tibet's staple food made of roasted barley flour, and the traditional houses, where old men or young kids drew water into canisters from courtyard wells.

All the housing had courtyards, surrounded by three or four foot high stone walls. This was where the domestic animals stayed, ponies, mules, cattle, and all the walls had holes for the animals to wander in and out. The large, extended families lived behind doors in individual quarters within the compound.

A cadre worked under his truck, then jumped in and drove off. We went back to wait for our boys. There was no cold beer in Tinggri because there was no electricity in Tinggri.

We sat in the LandCruiser until mouth-breathers, miscreants and beggars surrounded us and stared in the windows. I went in to round up our team, who sat on long wooden benches in the darkened room. They said ok, ok, one minute. A cooking fire flared in a room behind a curtain, and lit up a half dozen men in the shadows, smoking.

I went back after fifteen minutes. Everybody smoked and talked over butter tea. Our driver was just being served a bowl of noodles.

Pissed me off. I told them we had to go and stood there while he gobbled and slurped. My audacity, to haul them out of there after their hour and a half noodle break, sowed the seeds of destruction.

•••••

For half the day we drove through canyons, along an escarpment and through an absolutely gorgeous painted desert. Finally I just put away my camera, convinced I couldn't even start to capture all the magnificence.

Dry, still, crisp and hot. An utterly clear sky. Almost nobody was in sight anywhere, except for our company from back in Tinggri. After lunch, out at the edge of town, our boys made some phrases about, "she is going to Xegar," and in popped an elfin Tibetan woman of forty, who settled into the back of the LandCruiser on top of our bags. She coughed a lot.

So, okay, we were off with a hackin' chick in the trunk and sullen staff in front. We got some slow Indian tunes on the juke. Between Tinggri and Xegar was ruggedly beautiful, in an unsettling, Tibetan way. Dusty. We rolled our windows down for the breeze except when trucks approached, kicking up dust.

Just before Xegar stood an imbecilic checkpoint where we waited on the side of the road in the LandCruiser while the local three we'd accrued scampered off into a little squat building that sat, I mean, in the middle of absolutely slap-me-blind nowhere.

Now, man may do worse things to man than to restrict movement in a place so utterly barren, vast and empty, but hardly anything more stupid. So many rules in a place so empty.

•••••

The wind howled as we climbed beyond Xegar, past settlements not on the map. The first power lines connected to the east, to Lhasa and the grid, were just wooden poles with two wires strung along them. We still had our hitchhiker, even past Xegar.

Where it had been hot in Tinggri, now it turned frigid again. For some hours we passed only a single, lone horseman.

Sometime past three, the engine just stopped and the boys climbed back under the hood. The police happened to motor up going the other way (a miracle!), but they just looked, backed up and went around. Didn't offer any help.

You can get used to most anything, I guess, and we got accustomed to piling in and out of the LandCruiser for mechanical reasons. The first time we sat on rocks our hackin' mama shared Lao Lao Tang bubble gum with Mirja and me. Then we set out across another rock field, did maybe twelve minutes and sputtered again.

The first time your car breaks down in the third world is de rigueur. The second time, if necessary, is included in the package. But we began to sense a routine.

Heavy patches of ice hung along either side of the road. At the next pass, even higher than before at 5200 meters, we felt much less altitude sickness. The only peak, and it was dominant, stood in snowy splendor. I asked its name.

Now, way back at the border, when we were happy to get a ride, we got both our "helper's" and driver's names. Since then, I'd lost so much faith in the Han helper bastard, and talked with him so little that I forgot his name, and our driver's too, and I didn't care.

I named our driver "Noodleboy" in honor of lunch at Tinggri and I just called our little monolingual "helper," "Sir." Sir asked Noodleboy what the name of the peak was, they talked, and Sir turned to me, "No special name."

We sputtered to a stop twice more. Let me tell you, that one last time I was frustrated. The LandCruiser idled low but Noodleboy didn't know to shift out of fourth when we'd brake to ease through streams. He wouldn't apply gas, the engine would die, and we'd all hop out and into our routines.

When we stalled right in the middle of a creek and a bus pulled up, blocked by us, somebody asked, "How long you been here?"

I told them don't worry, they'll fix it in fifteen minutes, they've been doing it all day. The people on the bus thought that was a lot funnier than I did.

•••••

Boys wearing Mao-caps drove past on those rototiller-like trucks. I sat and wondered at the geography - the really awesome upthrust rocks, almost to vertical, caused by the collision of the Indian and Asian tectonic plates. Plus, I wasn't busy.

Then I'd wonder about us. I marveled at the time, money and effort we spent chasing the allure of the vacant, slack-jawed peasant, like, well, our very own Noodleboy.

And unkindly, I wondered how a driver could be so dense as to not grasp even the basics of his job, in this case like the concept of the downshift, or how to press the gas pedal to rev the engine.

I asked if I could drive and they just laughed.

One other thing about Noodleboy: Except to pass, he drove on the left, even when the left was a precipice, even in fourth gear approaching the crest of a hill. All the time. The whole trip. Every minute. In Tibet driving is on the right.

•••••

Once when we were broken down, a LandCruiser with three Europeans and a Real English-Speaking Guide stopped to help. I explained to the Real English-Speaking Guide how Noodleboy would let the engine die and he talked it over with Noodleboy and Sir, but nothing changed. That LandCruiser followed along with us for a while, as if to rescue us if our LandCruiser finally gave up.

This slowed them down considerably. Finally, at one repair stop, one Euro-guy slammed the door and theatrically started walking ahead into the desert (where was he going?)

and I was secretly with Noodleboy when eventually we thundered by him and covered him with dust.

Just part of the routine.

It was fifteen minutes to Lhaze, Sir declared. Forty-five minutes later when we asked how far now, he pondered and offered brightly, "about forty kilometers."

There was one last checkpoint. Just beyond it we had a flat tire.

Which was the crystalline moment between exasperation and acceptance. What had been a bad day was becoming a tolerably good story. So right there on the rocks by the road Mirja and the hitchhiker and I broke out the Bagpiper India whiskey carefully imported from Banepa, Nepal and toasted our boys fixing the tire.

Our hitchhiker showed us pictures of her two daughters, and her Dalai Lama amulet, so I slid her one of my smuggled Dalai Lama postcards. In gratitude, when we finally rolled up to Lhaze, she carried one of our bags and asked for a dollar.

•••••

In Lhaze, I was the American son-of-a-bitch who wrote the book on being a jerk. That's what our driving team thought, because I had made them hurry through their noodles back at lunch. I thought they were no-account bastards who couldn't organize a drive across their own goddam country.

So we had a lot to build on for tomorrow.

I pointed to the flat spare and asked if it would get fixed. They said it would. We agreed to leave for Xigatse at 8:00 tomorrow morning and the boys vanished.

A young girl with a radiant smile led us up the stairs by flashlight, down the hall to our room. They had power, but not until eight o'clock.

Not much use being there unable to see, so we found a restaurant across the street, where there was power, and talked with some men from Guangdong on their way to China's Everest base camp for holiday.

We asked for cold beer and one of the guys tried to translate. The waitress looked puzzled, was gone too long, then came back smiling triumphantly, buckling under a big metal tub of raw meat. Our translator thought we asked for "cold beef."

A little boy did his best to burn the place down firing up a propane lantern to augment the bare bulb above us. Now that it was getting dark, the power worked intermittently. A table full of card playing boys from Szechuan province came in to wash their hands in a pot on the main floor.

One man saw a book I had opened to a page about the Tashilunpo Monastery in Xigatse and grabbed it from my hands. I slid him a Dalai Lama card and he grabbed it, too, and in an instant slipped it out of sight and into his inside coat pocket. They cooked up what smelled like breakfast sausage and it smelled great.

Back across the street we purified water and made Thai chicken and fried rice from backpacker's kits and had a little party. The moon was near new, it was so dark and the stars couldn't have been brighter. On the way to the toilet (which was outside), I smiled at Orion.

Noise continued late into the night, kind sounds, singing and laughing.

•••••

First thing in the morning the troubles started again.

Eight o'clock, agreed time, we're on the gravel by the car. Our helper, Sir, showed up on time, loaded our stuff and said now, they were going to breakfast. I walked with him a ways, put my hands on both his shoulders and tried to explain.

A smoking Chinese boy in a cheap suit interrupted, "I need to talk to him."

I said I was talking to him.

"Oh, you are special person!" His voice rose derisively.

This was going great.

We waited. About 8:30 the boys re-emerged with our hackin' chick in tow. She'd be going with us - and they hadn't fixed the spare, and they never did.

On the road, Mirja tried banter.

"It was loud last night. Was...there...party?"

Pause. Blank look.

"Karaoke maybe?" She tried again.

Recognition.

"Karaoke, yeah."

"Do they do that every night?"

"Every night, yeah."

•••••

There was no electricity in the hotel in the morning, but it still felt closer to civilization than the day before amid the nomads.

One of those ubiquitous blue Chinese trucks threw up dust ahead so we couldn't see for several kilometers, as we climbed out of a dry, gray gravel gulch. Peaceful, empty landscape scrolled by for an hour and more. Cooking fires rose from settlements and streams glinted in the slant of the early morning sun.

A mantra carved in giant characters stretched across a hillside. Gradually, a few at a time, trees popped up around settlements - but only around the settlements. Then a thick stand of trees lined a riverbank. Ten army transport trucks convoyed by. More yaks. A dust devil out in a field.

A series of long valleys stretched to the horizon, then again, and again. Snow patches dotted the stark brown hills and clouds would form, little cumulus puffs, out of mere air. Riding along, you could just sit and watch them, and with a long horizon and plenty of time, that's just what we did. A sing-along broke out to the cassettes. A happy few hours.

•••••

Xigatse is Tibet's second city, former home of the Panchen Lama. His residence, the Tashilunpo Monastery, is one of the few monasteries the Chinese tolerate. The Tashilunpo Monastery and the best hotel in Tibet outside Lhasa both gave Xigatse a certain allure. So when we pulled up to Friendship Hotel #2 instead of our promised and paid for Xigatse hotel - the one with the toilets - the whole tenuous peace broke down.

I insisted we must go the Xigatse Hotel. Sir, our "helper," turned around full to talk to us for the very first time, and Noodleboy mouth-breathed faster. Sir exploded.

For the first time, in his anger, he made himself understood. I had done a bad thing when I came in and dragged them away from their friends at lunch. All Chinese eat lunch! He was just doing his job.

He showed me a list of the amounts of money he'd been given back at the border for our lodging. It included 120 yuan, or $15 for today. The Xigatse Hotel was 480, or $60, and he couldn't pay for that.

He didn't know how we did it in our country but in Tibet they did it the Chinese way. He angrily decided: He'd give us the 120, we could stay wherever we liked. No monastery tour for us today and tomorrow we leave for Lhasa at 8:00 sharp!

That was what we wanted, too. So once everybody cooled off they drove us over there and Sir insisted on theatrically unloading my bag, admonished "8:00 tomorrow" and they all stormed away.

We were pretty happy with that.

•••••

After a Xigatse walking tour I felt there was nothing clean in Tibet. It's one thing among nomads, or in towns with no electricity (forget plumbing), but here in the second city every sidewalk smelled of piss - every single one - and so did the famous Tashilunpo monastery.

One monk-boy there begged for money - kind of in contravention of monkhood, I thought - and at the free market outside the monastery adult women had this irritating way of insistently laying on your arm begging for the entire length of the market.

The monastery was superlative though, majestic on a hill, a warren of cobbled alleyways and cooled out dogs in the sun. It made your heart pound to climb the steps. I climbed up some maintenance stairs inside the main gate to get a picture of the whole complex and a furious monk hurried over to accost me.

Tashilunpo Monastery, Xigatse.

Mirja noted, "Now you've pissed off two Tibetans in one day – and one of them was a monk."

It was a glorious, beautiful spring day. The leaves were young and green and the sun burned your skin in just an hour. Maybe it was the nicest single day I have ever been in - except that the next day was just as nice.

•••••

I wasn't giving them any excuse. I watched the sun's first rays strike the prayer flags on the hill behind Tashilunpo monastery from the cool of the front of the Xigatse hotel at 8:00 sharp. They weren't there. By 8:20 I was pretty discouraged and by 8:40 I found a tour bus driver who made me understand he was leaving for Lhasa at 10:00 - but I didn't know how to ask him if he had room for us.

By 8:45 I was in a back office trying to raise Lhasa over the phone when Mirja called down the hall that they were here. Off we went, including the hackin' chick, who was on a free ride all the way to Lhasa.

As a second city, much as I'd like to, I can't say Xigatse impressed very much. Outside the Panchen Lama's headquarters there was only the barren, blue-collar, grappling feel of a hardscrabble frontier town.

•••••

The closer to Lhasa, the more prayer flags. I had begun to think the whole of Tibetan spirituality was a western canard when we were out on the plateau, but now you could see it.

The road out of Xigatse was smooth for a long time and the day was as beautiful as you'll ever see. We'd heard all the music the boys had by now and started it again. That was what Sir, our "helper," helped with most - tape changing.

Mesas and mini-plateaus, eroded flat, stood alongside the tarmac road. No snow on the hills, no grazing animals. From a high vantage point, range after high range lined up ever more distant.

Like the day before, trees lined the creeks, and now settlements were surrounded by planted trees. Mule carts still plied the roads, and people walked along with shovels and farm tools. The Yalong River stretched wide, reflecting the big blue sky. Then came high tension wires. Signs at a construction sight were in Chinese only, no Tibetan. A fence inexplicably walled off an empty quarter on the right.

Credit to the hackin' chick: We rode with her for three days and on each of them, while she wore the same outfit (in fact she carried no bags), she was always fresh. While the boys wore cheap western-style clothes made in China, she wore a native blue print blouse and cotton vest with her long skirt covered by an apron. She kept her hair bunned up with a blue headband. And she plied us with Chinese caramels.

Carrying water from the spring.

Sheep and snow again. A fascinating winch-ferry system hauled people and animals across the Yalong River. At four separate places.

Following the Yalong valley, I spent the morning watching the cumulus and the countryside. At eleven that morning, I couldn't have been happier, feeling the breeze, watching the green river turn white over rocks as we maneuvered through towering mountains.

We stopped in a village high on a hill surrounded by tall snow-capped mountains. Yaks were being put out while women filled silver urns with water at the spring, and prayer flags flapped over the river.

Then (after they got the Toyota restarted) we hurtled headlong into a valley. Long haired goats. More prayer flags. Even as we broke down a few more times it really was so beautiful (and we were close enough to Lhasa) that we'd already put our boys in past tense and just looked forward to a couple of days off the road.

•••••

How many Tibetans does it take to fill a gas tank? Seven, and fifteen minutes, at Changkong/Beijing station sixty kilometers from Lhasa. That didn't include fascinated onlookers - or the fifteen extra minutes and two more Tibetans to restart your LandCruiser.

•••••

Albania to Zimbabwe, Noodle Boy was the worst driver we've ever had. He really would shift from third to fourth while meaning to accelerate to pass. I fear he may just have been a major, base dullard - nothing more. It's mean but it may also be true.

Sir never got the concept of the client-provider relationship. Most places people understand that if you pay something, you expect something in return. Except this guy. He was a young Han Chinese man working at the edge of the empire. Maybe he fashioned himself as contributor to a great enterprise, taming the heathen.

He wanted us to go with him to his travel agency boss, a Dutchman, who he thought would make it all right. I lied that we'd call his boss once we checked into our hotel in Lhasa, and once Lhasa rolled into view, we found our hotel, piled out, they wished us a good stay in Tibet, and all of us, I think, wished we'd acted better.

•••••

12 PARAGUAY

The farthest back water washes to a national capital must be Asuncion, Paraguay. It's as if its residents didn't ask for the honor, but the capital had to be somewhere so they amiably accommodated.

Maybe parts of Africa are less vital. Think Ouagadougou, maybe, or Bangui. Even somnambulant Vientiane, which is in Laos, shows more vitality than here, smack in the middle of South America.

They'd rolled up the streets by the time we installed ourselves in the Sabe Hotel. The front desk spoke not so much as "hello." No English. Here in the national capital.

The TV wouldn't work until tomorrow because it was New Years Day and they couldn't get anybody out to fix it, but it was a nice enough place. A picture hung partly over the window in the hallway. That was a little strange.

I was out early in the morning, through the business district and down to the Paraguay River. It wasn't very big, downtown Asuncion, and it wasn't very busy.

There was the main Plaza de los Heroes, down a few blocks, and Asuncion had a building modeled after the Pantheon. Sales ladies' tables along Avenue Palma offered up the usual languid market fare: watches and underwear and (allegedly) Nike clothes and plastic toys. Birds were loud and it was hot hot hot by 8:45.

Down at the river, General Francisco Solana Lopez's white-washed mansion, started in 1860, stood shuttered. Beyond it, children pumped water at a clutter of squatter shacks. A sand spit stretched out to two rusting shipwrecks, resting over on their sides, just on the edge of the water. Here in the national capital.

The breathtaking Asuncion waterfront.

But let's start at the beginning, which was a few days earlier.

The Girl from Ipanema and her ilk played from speakers in the stone-floored breakfast room at the Triple Borders, where Argentina, Brazil and Paraguay meet, a place that keenly interested the U.S. after September 11th, because the government was convinced terrorists operated, or at least laundered money there.

As Kelly Hearn told the story in the Christian Science Monitor in 2005, a motorcycle taxi driver in Cuidad del Este shouted "from inside his helmet: 'They want to control all this. They think terrorists are here.'

'They' means the US military."

Hearn wrote, "Before and immediately after 9/11, US officials suspected that Al Qaeda was active in the so-called Triple Border area where Paraguay, Argentina, and Brazil meet. Those fears have dwindled to allegations that Arab businessmen in Ciudad del Este use profits from pirated goods to fund Middle East terrorist groups. The Brazilian government has estimated that $6 billion of illegal funds are wired out of Ciudad del Este annually."

•••••

On the Argentina side of the border at Iguazu Falls, it was so bloody hot every day, how could you smuggle? We just watched the wildlife. We only ever saw a fraction, but there were tons: Escorpiones and coleopterous beetles that grew to tablespoon size – they stood an inch high. Scary, but turn 'em over and they just wiggle.

There were aranas, tarantulas, and eighty billion mosquitoes. Monkeys and sloths and the tamandua lived in trees. The tamandua ate honey. The carpincho, I think it wasn't sure if it was a beaver or an anteater. And the lobo gargantilla didn't know if it was a beaver or an eel, with fat swimmers' feet and an ugly tube of a body, four feet long with its tail.

The tiny deerlike corzuela enana had no chance against a six foot alligator called nombre vulgar. There was the tegu lizard – Mirja saw one - and porcupines, little cats and orange-billed toucans and toucans both verde and amarillo. The most famous big cats, pumas and yaguaretes, were nowhere to be found. Must have been way back in the jungle. There was a little museum where a yaguarete was chomping down on a tapir.

Armadillos were the most unfortunate. Everybody ate them, even big lizards. On the other hand, anteaters must taste awful. Nobody ate them but the big cats. And there was tree-sized bamboo thick as the top of your arm, everywhere you looked.

•••••

A man named Walter drove us over to the Brazilian side of the falls across the River Paraná. On the strength of Walter vouching for us that we'd be back in Argentina later that same day, that didn't require a border stop.

But we were going on through Brazil for Paraguay. Walter said we'd need a visa and tomorrow was a holiday, consulate was closed, so we went to the Brazilian consulate in Argentina right then. It took just twenty minutes, even typing on a manual typewriter, because no one was there but us. That amazed Walter. He said it usually takes at least an hour.

Walter Foerster's folks moved to Argentina as kids just about the time their parents would have been fleeing Germany in the wake of World War Two. That was pretty common in Chile, Argentina, Brazil and Paraguay. The president of Paraguay for thirty years was the son of an immigrant brewer, a man named Alfredo Stroessner.

In the Iguaçu National Park, in Brazil, black-fringed yellow butterflies threw themselves by the thousands at Walter's Peugeot. Nandus, cousin to ostriches, stood in a preserve. Anteaters pilfered tourists' ice cream cones along a walkway skirting the hammering torrents of Iguazu Falls.

It was good not to speak the language.

The kids whined, "Papa I've got to pee" and the adults were sniping like the wife of Kurt down in Patagonia, but if you couldn't understand them, you could pretend they were comparing impressions of the aesthetics of such a volume of moving water.

•••••

Foz de Iguaçu, Brazil was a city of 300,000, with orange-drink hawkers at every traffic light, and these lights were cool, too, not just one red and one green, but a whole scheme-full of reds and greens, five apiece in columns. When the color changed the top one was lit, and the less time left, the lower the light slid toward the bottom until the color changed again.

Foz boasted a couple of mid-rise buildings, the Itabon sushi bar, billboards for cell phones advertising "100 minutas gratis," and an Avenue Schimmelpfing. There were residential towers that had never been finished, and the TV Cataratas tower stood back from the road, inside Agriculture Ministry property.

Foz de Iguaçu, Brazil.

There were the Oklahoma Texaco and the Antarctica Restaurant, and across the street, Bar Mania. They had a thing for Mona Lisa around here: A Mona Lisa Hotel in Foz, and signs advertising duty free shopping at Mona Lisa shopping center across the border in Paraguay.

We checked the bus schedules to Paraguay and they didn't really suit us: three times a day, at 00:05, 7:00 and 18:05. The 18:05 wasn't A/C, and it would put us at the bus station in Asuncion after midnight with hotel reservations at a hotel that (we didn't know yet) didn't exist.

Walter told me how much most people paid for a private car to Asuncion while we stood there in the bus station, and when I said okay, he drove us back to Argentina and he was quiet and stroked his chin and I thought he might want to make that money for himself. And sure enough he did.

Walter and his Peugeot were ready the next afternoon at 1:30 and whisked us out of Iguazu. We stopped for border stamps at Argentina and Brazil and motored straight on to Cuidad del Este, Paraguay's second city.

•••••

Walter warned that we might lose our film if we took pictures of the border, but eating chicken out of a box interested the border police more than we did. There was an advantage to traveling on the New Years Day holiday. We were the only people trying to get in and Walter was ecstatic, because it can take an hour or two there, but this only took about three minutes.

Disappointing, predictable Cuidad del Este, Paraguay's East City, squatted in the sun, poor and dusty and ramshackle, low buildings crumbling into lumps along the highway, traffic lights out and money changers in leather money belts glowering on the side of the road. Walter stopped, didn't like the rate, then did a deal at the Esso for fifty Argentina pesos worth of Guarani. And we were off for Asuncion.

Walter was a big man. He had to open the Peugeot's door and stick his leg out to get the money out of his pocket. I thought it was unlikely he could spend those pesos unless it was for gas.

In Cuidad del Este you longed to be out in the country again. A John Deere heavy equipment store, red dirt, no landscape and litter. You'd think there was a competition to see how foul they could make the roadside. Men with guns sat on stools. On the other side of town they'd torn up the road and didn't appear to have plans to fix it.

The caballeros barracks was the nicest building in Cuidad del Este. Mirja imagined that if you were a young man living in the dirt, it might make you want to join.

It was as humid as it gets, just sopping drippy. We and others double-passed some of the slower cars on the two lane road which, if nothing else superlative can be said, was in tolerably good shape all the way to Asuncion. Good enough to speed.

Somewhere a road wandered off to the left. A sign with an arrow read "Novotel 247K."

New Year picnics had the rural population of eastern Paraguay out in their front yards just like they might be anywhere in the rural U.S. south – guys in their undershirts, everybody in flip flops. They sat in twos and fives in lawn chairs under trees.

To move was to sweat, but still some played the odd volleyball game. A funeral procession moved slowly alongside the road on foot, a cluster of men carrying a simple wooden coffin on their shoulders.

Here was a girl with a bag on her head as big as she was, there was a stickball game. Red dirt and dust everywhere, and people at every water hole. Tethered cattle. Roosters. Hippodromos. And Gomerias (tire repair shops).

There were so many Gomerias that I got cross at seeing them. I mean, really, every kilometer or so for five hours, a tire sat out at the road painted with the word "Gomeria." You either don't need anything to set up a Gomeria or maybe there was a government subsidy if you did. That's it, the government must pay people to own Gomerias so they can be in the record book as "Proud Paraguay - home of the world's most Gomerias."

Paraguayans didn't honk their horns. Well, okay, there's not much traffic, but that doesn't stop the rest of the third world's drivers. Here in Paraguay, it was quiet.

Out in the country we'd occasionally roll past carts with chest-high wagon wheels, and pigs, granaries, geese and people in the open backs of trucks. Lots of the old original Volkswagen beetles. There weren't too many potholes and I was surprised.

Roofs were terra cotta or tin, wells built of brick. Grafitti: "Ricardo y Fatty C." A car sped by us with the license plate: "Georgia Bulldogs."

Colinas (hills) sprang up two hundred kilometers out of Asuncion. A horse wandered too close to the road. The highway stretched ten kilometers ahead, flat and straight, and cumulus appeared on the horizon. The first clouds of the day.

Towns now, not dirty outposts like Cuidad del Este, but proper little villages with centers and trees. 86 K from Asuncion, one town was open for business, stores, shops, kids on motorbikes and police on patrol. They put short, three-cornered stools – like in Rangoon - out by the roadside. White cloth on top kept chipas, cheese buns, warm.

Nearer Asuncion wealth was more manifest, cattle and sheep, and farms well tended with well-maintained roads. For a while there was a passing lane.

It remained unrelentingly hot, with grassy-topped palms and wild cactus. Vendors sold bananas or garlic. Toward the big city, you could buy baseball caps and underwear by the roadside, and one sign advertised "Sex Toys." Signs supplied by advertisers like Bremen beer lit a few shops, and always there were Gomerias.

More colinas. 48 kilometers out the highway divided and the river Paraguay came into view. You could sail to the Atlantic from here, the Paraguay River to the Paraná to the Plata (I guess you'd have to put out and walk around Iguazu Falls), so that you'd finally sail into the ocean between Buenos Aires and Montevideo.

Two names I enjoyed: The Juan O'Leary bus line, and in the town of Loranzo, the clinic of Dr. Jose Rosenbaum.

The race was on to get to town before dark. I started out thinking that was a lock but Walter was ever the courteous driver, even timid, after a lifetime of driving in the small towns around Iguazu, and as the tempo picked up toward Asuncion, he hung back. And there was the little matter of him not knowing his way. We cruised cheesy neighborhoods on the outskirts, Walter showing manly reluctance to ask directions.

After he'd asked once, though, he'd stop every four minutes to ask again. I don't know how he handled his Spanish conversations, but when he talked with us, Walter would typically start in his best stab at English and invariably end in Spanish, mumbling.

He was a perfectly nice fellow, maybe a little small-town slack-jawed, and it was a pleasure having him drive us into Paraguay, although I didn't envy his turning around and driving back down that five hour highway in the dark. Finally, with the sun behind some of the downtown buildings, we found the hotel.

Just the tiniest problem: it was out of business. The Guarani, the best in town in the "Official Hotel Guide," had its windows shuttered, no sign and a police guard. This had happened just recently, obviously, because there was a Christmas tree in the lobby, and we were never made to know what was really up. It was a twinge disconcerting when we drove up to see the man who tried to help us look so pitifully sorry for us.

Whatever had happened, we asked for the best hotel in town and they showed us to it, and that was the Hotel Sabo, just around a couple of corners, and it must've had a half dozen guests on fourteen floors, so there was really no problem.

Asuncion may be the world's least interesting capital city, but that's not to say it's mean. It's really just a simple place filled with agreeable, unassuming people. It's set on gentle hills, and I remember ten years before, I knew a man who had gone to adopt a baby in Asuncion. He was the only person I'd ever known who'd been to Paraguay and I asked him what it was like.

"Beautiful," he'd told me, and I wondered what Paraguay he'd been to. It's not beautiful, but it's not ugly either. Really, it's just a simple place with agreeably unassuming people, none of whom speak any English.

At a place called Itaugua down the road from Asuncion, known for it's spider-web style lace, Mirja had a manicure/pedicure for two bucks while I walked through the dust and watched the horsemen and brightly painted buses until I found Bar Himalaya and had a couple beers. The temperature gauge hit 41 degrees (105.7F) on the way into town. It was so flippin' hot that they served half litre beers iced in champagne buckets, with a glass. Elegance, Paraguayan style.

The Itaugua bus enters the Pan-American highway.

On Saturdays in Asuncion, most of the shops just simply didn't reopen after siesta. Restaurant Bolsi was a good choice for dinner in large part because it was open. Walking down to the Plaza de los Heroes, where Restaurant Bolsi is, loud music streamed from all the shops that were open. Saturday night.

Saturday night or not, dogs lay about in the middle of the street. Street vendors sat at their carts with no customers. Those who were open were liable to be watching a tiny black and white TV propped inside their carts.

The feeling on the dark streets was the approximate opposite of danger. Our most risqué moment was walking past a knot of six girl prostitutes in tight pants, smoking and talking on a street corner. Never, even in the fading light that first night where the police had shut down our hotel, did we ever feel anything but welcome.

At Restaurant Bolsi they sat us down and set us up with our champagne bucket of beer and brought out cups of chicken bouillon. We were only the third table in the place, but that changed. Paraguayans do the Latin late dining thing.

Corn meal biscuits, not exactly cornbread, were delicious.

Now you're right, when you visit a place and one of the things you remark on is the corn meal biscuits, it's possible it's not be the world's hottest spot. Asuncion may not be very interesting, but its citizens are carefree. Maybe you needn't visit. But if you lived there, you'd be happy.

•••••

A Fokker 100 took us home, operated by TAM, which is an acronym for something like Transportes Aereos del Mercosur, Mercosur being the economic union down here like NAFTA and the EU.

Felices Fiestas. Over the badlands (I don't know if they're called that but they ought to be, exactly the monotonous same from above like the Australian outback) they came up the aisle and handed out Papa Noel Christmas ornaments.

Six Catholic sisters, who obviously didn't fly much, joined us on this TAM flight. Grim at takeoff, they loosened up and they were all smiles and camera flashes by the end. The pilots showed kids (and sisters) the cockpit.

They asked, in English, "Would you like another beer, sir?" – a sentence never spoken in U.S. air space.

There was some prize raffle. We didn't understand it in Spanish, but they would call out seat numbers and people would clap and someone would run up to the front to claim their prize. One of the sisters even won. And when we landed in Chile everybody in the plane clapped.

•••••

13 BORNEO

A fine young man with a Yesus Kristus medallion bouncing around beneath his mirror drove us the seven or so kilometers into Mt. Kinabalu park, through the sleeping village of Kundasang. Farmers congregated at a warren of tin-roofed stalls along the main road. It looked like a good day for green tomatoes, potatoes, and cabbage.

They hauled us all in bas minis from the ranger station to the trailhead. From there, a six-kilometer trail led up to our destination, the Laban Ratah guest house, at 11,000 feet. At 13,432 feet, Mt. Kinabalu's summit, in Malaysian Borneo, is the highest point in Southeast Asia.

The first kilometer (the trail was marked at each 1/2 kilometer) popped by in 23 minutes. We were flyin', and all that stuff about how hard this would be was just talk. The first kilometer, we only stopped long enough to shed our wraps.

Just at first the trail led downhill, charming, to a cool, wet place called Carson's Falls. On the way down the mountain, conversely, having to climb at the end was just one last kick in the butt on the way out the door.

Still before 8:00 a.m. no sunlight had fought its way to the forest floor. The air was downright chilly once our shirts turned sweaty. And they did — at the first K marker they weren't soaked through, but a breeze blew down the rise and chilled our damp skin.

We were cocky, jaunty, making tracks, and unappreciative of the flora, except the little violet flower of the Kinabalu Balsam, which was shaped more like it had a beard than lower petals.

The massif stood silent and still, the only sounds birds or a rustling squirrel. There are no monkeys on Mt. Kinabalu. They live nearer the sea, to the east.

The Summit of Mt. Kinabalu, 13,435 feet.

Our guide Erik was a volcano of phlegm at first, hacking, spitting, coughing, exercising all facial cavities. He was a little guy, as these highland people were, but with the strong, imposing legs you'd imagine.

He guided once a week, reckoned he'd done the climb fifty times. His personal record to the top — a place called Low's Peak — was about three hours.

The rest of the week he helped his parents haul their produce to the Kundasang market, where you cain't make no money. Erik said a kilo of cabbage brought fourteen U.S. cents.

•••••

Grim realization set in during kilometer two. I felt my pack with every step, even though all it held was a camera, a towel, a dry t-shirt, bread, cheese and water.

We appreciated the moss, ferns and banana trees and searched for these particular birds who sang in two notes, but a little more grimly, a little less buoyant, quieter. Still, we made two kilometers in 58 minutes, and there were only six, total. We fed the squirrels some of the tiny peanuts Mirja had bought. Still cool and still, the entire third kilometer. Dark, thick, jungly, even almost cold, and about an hour and a half after we'd set out, at two minutes to nine, we marked halfway.

•••••

In the fourth kilometer, blazing red running shorts caught my gaze. I looked up from the path and it was a Japanese fellow, smiling. He made the summit, turned, and passed us on his way back down before we'd made four and a half K. I just couldn't believe that.

They do this run as competition. The winner last year, Ian Holmes of the U.K., did 21 K up to the peak and back in 2:43:20, trailed by fellow Brit Simon Booth at 2:43:22. Poor Simon Booth.

•••••

I thought of Beck Weathers on that famous ill-fated Everest expedition, who was left for dead, but stumbled, frostbitten, back to camp. He said mountain climbing, really, was simple. All you had to do was be in shape and then not let your mind defeat your body. One foot in front of the other, he said, it's all just endurance.

But by now I was grim, unhappy, soaked-through wet. I used Weathers' advice and eventually thought I'd achieved a sort of runner's high. I had a little bounce back, but I was hiking sloppy — lurching, and, when there was something to grab on to, I hauled myself up by it. Still, I was sure for the first time since Carson's Falls that we would make it. I turned cocky.

We stopped to enjoy Mirja's chocolates and tiny peanuts, like they sell in Nuwara Eliya, back in Sri Lanka. We sat there steaming. Our own personal dew points produced our own, individual, self-generated clouds of steam, our shirts purely drenched through.

•••••

Porters made good money — six ringgits per kilo — but that work's just too hard, Erik thought, and I was sure he was right. A typical load was ten to twelve kilos (twenty max) and that'd bring you twenty bucks — then you had to haul the trash back down from the top.

Erik liked guiding.

U.S. twenty was real money. The park required we have a guide and took a fee for him, so that Erik made about eight bucks for his day, probably as good as a porter if he got a right-tipping foreigner — and no taking out the trash.

The porters plied the path up and back, right alongside us, low to the ground and bent, exchanging local-language intelligence with Erik on the way, usually hauling rice bags full of supplies for the restaurant and guest houses up above, held by straps across their foreheads. Or sometimes they'd be laden with daypacks and duffels of tourists.

Twice we passed Japanese girls in flip-flops, and the last one was really hobbling, on her boyfriend's arm. Mountain climbing may involve stepping over rocks. Apparently they were not told.

•••••

Erik commanded pretty good English.

Had he ever been to K. L. (Kuala Lumpur, the capital)? I asked.

"No, but when I get money I take my baby."

It's a big city, you know, tallest building in the world (at the time)....

"Oh, no!" Scornful reply. He was aiming high. "Maybe one day I get 10,000 ringgits I go around the world!"

•••••

I spent long minutes anticipating the sun, by which to energize. We were still deep within the forest at the two-hour mark, and again I had begun to flag. It was damp, I was wet, and the path stretched only straight up.

Twenty or thirty meters of steep steps would lead to a bend, and you'd yearn for a stretch that didn't lead straight up, but time after time after time after time after time, you'd reach the bend and see even crueler steps beyond. And then you'd do it again. And then again.

•••••

At first the sun would hit the forest floor in this odd spot or that, then as we rose (so slowly) up the hill you'd see sun more often than not, and by 10:00 in the morning we stood at the Layang Layang staff hut, on a little plateau flooded by sunlight. I drenched my head under a water pipe.

Up to now there were few on the mountain with us except the runner and a couple of porters. Now groups of overnight campers passed us bound for the bottom, but no one but Malay boys climbed (in fact, we were the first to set out, and first to arrive at Laban Rata).

Eric was constant. Mirja and I waxed and waned at intervals, and kept one another going. At the four K mark, I hit my stride one last time. It was 10:08, only two K to go. I fairly strode ahead. The sun was out now, but we'd ever be ducking into a crook in the trail that led through shaded forest.

Here was a sign, "NEPENTHES VILLOSA areas 9000-10,300 ft." by which they meant those curious pitcher plants were about, and we spied several in the woods, the biggest the size of two fists.

The curious pitcher plant.

A big Chinese contingent slid downward, all chatty. Along about here my recently found vigor ran out and I resented their being able to breathe. Like Mirja said, on the way up it's your heart and lungs, on the way down it's your legs, and I began to get an ugly payback for my cocky "hitting my stride" bit, as I could hear my heart pounding in my head.

We stopped (it was an excuse to stop) to watch a green bird, the "Mt. Kinabalu Blackeye."

•••••

Now this was terrible. Stretching above us we had to begin some scrambling. It was just damned hard. Mud. I saw myself closed off now, thinking only of where my next foot would go (except I had this vague "What the hell were you thinking!?" notion bouncing around my head, too).

I seized upon a mantra. I said to myself, over and over, "Mt. Kinabalu blackeye." Over and over. Now, whenever we'd spy anyone above us on the trail, we'd ("graciously") stop to let them slide by.

One fifty-something Japanese fellow laughed at himself how he'd taken eight and a half hours to the summit. Hell, we weren't even going to the summit and we weren't laughing. Yeah, but anybody can laugh and climb down, I thought.

Now came a section where you had to haul yourself up by rope. Now the trees were small, dwarfed and gnarled by the wind, cold and thin air. They were small, but Erik said some were hundreds of years old.

At 10:58 we stood on the five K marker. Someone coming down asked if this was our first time and Mirja peremptorily replied, "And the last."

We could see the South China Sea from here, 52 kilometers to the north. And our hotel, the Perkassa, high on its hill overlooking Kundasang town, was an insignificant little speck below. We stopped every third or fourth step for the last kilometer, which took 50 minutes.

At 11:48 we reached the top.

Which wasn't the top. The Laban Rata guesthouse was built 15 years ago to support summit seekers. At 11,000 feet, it has 20 tables, bunks and a grocery with Milo, old batteries, candy bars, Carlsbergs and a kitchen serving up fried rice, sweet corn soup and coffee. The bulletin board admonished, though, that today we had no: cream of chicken soup, Maggi chicken, chicken, lemon or chicken curry. Cursed porters.

So we had lunch - fried rice - and climbed down. Four hours twenty minutes up, 3:10 down. On the way to the bottom we passed a mere boy carrying a 40 kg coil of rope. Impossible. Weak as I was by now, I couldn't even lift it, but he hoisted it through two loops onto his back and it would take a day and a half to haul it up there — for 63 dollars in ringgits.

We were both thoroughly hobbled by the last two K down, Mirja and me, our brakes having given out, both of us gripping the handrails when there were any, noticing all too clearly that Eric just ambled on down the hill ahead of us the way he had ambled up. We went home, ate a table full of daging redang and papadums with a side of fiery red chopped chillis, and slept hard by eight o'clock.

●●●●●

14 LAKE MALAWI

"On your right is area 50. This here is area 28, light industrial area. Across the road there is fertilizer factory and tobacco factory. That is heavy industrial area."

The national police headquarters came into view on the right.

"That is area 40."

Just across the street, "Area 43," Everlasting explained, "Is low industrial. It used to be only area ten, and area ten is still there, but it is full, so they have made area 43."

"We also have names but our names are too long, so we just say, say, area 12."

Malawi's Ministries stood on the left.

"So, is that area 1?"

Logical, I thought.

"No, that is area 20."

This went on all through Lilongwe.

"Ah, that is area 47. Up there, that's area 49. National Bank. Bank of the Nation." The tallest building in Malawi is the central bank.

"This is the Jehovah's Witness headquarters in Malawi."

•••••

When we met, our driver told us, "I am Everlasting." We sort of looked away, and then we realized that was his name.

Everlasting was a slow, deliberate speaker, easy enough to understand once you got acclimated. His "S's" kind of trailed off.

The Lilongwe River lolled by the market, near the old city administration building "from when Lilongwe was a small town." The new city hall, beacon of progress, had a "Ready Print" shop sign in a window on the second floor.

Everlasting showed us the flame tree, its red flower. What he called a tube tree at the central outdoor market, where a smiling little boy saw my camera and excitedly grabbed his friend's arm.

The mosque.

A few kilometers out of town, people along the roadside carried everything you could imagine. A stack of firewood, one guy with a dozen bright crimson pin wheels twirling in each hand.

"These people are coming back from the market. They have been selling."

They were Chewa, originally from Congo via Zambia, and among the longest settled Malawian tribes. Portuguese contact with the Chewa came as early as 1608, with evidence of the first Chewa kingdom just before the 1492 voyage of Columbus.

Everlasting began a lecture on goats: They should be tied so as not to eat the maize. Sometimes you cannot see where the goat is tied because the rope is so long. But sometimes the rope is gone away.

If you see a forest, Everlasting said, it is probably a cemetery. Village people cannot use cemetery land for growing, so, sensibly, they choose stands of forest for their burial grounds.

On a flagpole the national flag hung limp.

"The wind is not blowing so it is closed," Everlasting explained. Across the flag a red sun rose from the top of three bands, and Everlasting said that represents fire.

"The national team when they have done well we call them the Flames. When they have not, well, then it is silent."

When Everlasting got particularly involved in his stories, he'd punctuate his remarks with the car horn. Talkin' and tappin' and tootin'.

•••••

The lobola, or bride price, is not paid here. A boy goes to a girl's side and settles there. When they are blessed with children and they grow up to get married, the father cannot say no. That issue is referred to the boy's uncle.

So as an uncle myself, Everlasting told us, I must think of character – if the boy's family lives by fighting, for example, I might say no.

If we do not know the family well we can hire a spy to go and look at that family. The spy might test the boy to see if he will tell a lie. It may take a month.

The spy thing works both ways. His wife's family sent a spy to spy on Everlasting.

For the parents (and uncles), of course, it's all about character, not beauty.

"But for me as a boy, of course, I go for beauty." Everlasting was smiling.

That is in south and central region (where we were), Everlasting was at pains to point out. In the north district, we pay lobola. I have paid lobola for my wife.

Everlasting's wife cost four cows. She would cost considerably more today. If the cattle were too thin her family might say no, or okay, but you must pay something to help make the cattle fat. The lobola is 10 or 15 thousand kwacha now, he told us, but in those days it was four English pounds.

•••••

Lobola is a bridge between two families. Now Everlasting must care for his wife's mother and vice versa. And now he cannot divorce, or he would lose the lobola and the children (he said, in that order).

Not that he would. He was proud as any dad of his children, four boys and two girls. His son Harry was captain of the under 17 national football team, and Everlasting hoped he would play in the World Cup in South Africa.

We drove past a healer, "Herbalist of the Century – Zanga Phee," whose "Mult-Purpose Drug 1988 Centre" could handle "asthma, bp, cancer, diabetes, gout, jaundice, piles, ulcers and many more."

Zanga Phee, the Herbalist of the Century.

Zanga Phee drove Everlasting from his bride price reverie to make this point: At the regular hospital they had nothing. They got aspirin. But they had aspirin at home! So they'd go to a traditional healer to at least get something.

Everlasting's family said no to his first love. They sent him to tell her it was because they were distantly related, which was a lie, but nicer than telling her it was because she was Zambian.

•••••

Along the road a queue of women lined up in front of the maize mill holding baskets. Others, who had been through the mill, dried their production on mats. Maize makes sima, which is sticky grits.

Big sacks of cassava root lined the road. You can make cassava sima, and Everlasting maintained it's just as good as from maize.

•••••

As we moved further north we entered the land of the Yao (pronounced "Ya-wo"). There was a smaller Zulu tribe hereabouts, too, called Nguni. They were losers of a challenge to Chaka, the Zulu leader, and exiled as a result.

Forced from their homes, they fought under their leader Zwangendaba through Rhodesia, Mozambique, all the way north here to Nyasaland, the land of the lake people.

Finally the Bantu Yao, brandishing firearms supplied by Swahili-speaking Arab traders on the coast, checked the Nguni's northward spread, capturing and consigning some to slavery.

At their peak about 170 years ago, Arab traders from the coast moved as many as 20,000 slaves a year through the Lake Malawi port of Nkhotakota. The MV Ilala, with us aboard, would call at Nkhotakota two days later, from 3:00 to 5:00 in the morning, but in spite of the hustle and noise, neither of us woke.

•••••

A bridge was out on the most direct route from Lilongwe to the lake, so we swung south along the Mozambican border, and this brought us through the village of Kadambo.

"That house is in Mozambique."

"That tall tree there, it is in Mozambique."

"That goat is in Mozambique."

"The border is open. They are free to come and go," Everlasting explained, not condescending, but evincing a specific separateness.

"Some are our uncles. Some of us are their uncles. They sell in our markets. They use Malawian currency."

"This village was a refugee camp. Mozambique was a war-torn country. They build close to the border because they are afraid it will happen again."

On the road to Lake Malawi.

An expansive view opened up with our descent into the Great Rift Valley, stretching all the way out to Lake Malawi. There were mango and sausage trees and a particular acacia that actually fertilizes the soil ("See the maize near this tree is so green"), but Everlasting said it's unable to hold its leaves in rainy season and so appears dead.

These are mean people. Snakes stay away from people around here, Everlasting testified, because they know how dangerous these people are. When they see a snake they cannot go to bed until they kill it. The snakes know this.

Along the roadside baskets heaped full of mangoes for sale stood alongside bags of charcoal. Everlasting pointed out what must have been centuries-old baobab trees, at the rule of thumb of one meter of thickness per hundred years.

"The other way we differ, northerners and southerners, is the length of the handles," Everlasting was explaining.

He meant the handles of their hoes.

"In the south, they are bowing," Everlasting pointed out, indicating a man just there, in the field. This is because of their short handles.

"But we do not bow in the north. We have longer handles."

The northern tribes were historically more warlike, Everlasting posited, "So we cannot bow, we have to see."

•••••

Hastings Kamuzu Banda was the leader of Nyasaland at its independence as Malawi in 1964. He ruled until 1994. By 1993, under pressure and protest, President for Life Banda called presidential elections and was soundly defeated.

Guidebooks tell tales of travelers being forcibly given haircuts at the border, and quote this regulation from the 1970's:

"Female passengers will not be permitted to enter the country if wearing short dresses or trouser-suits, except in transit or at Lake Holiday resorts or National parks. Skirts and dresses must cover the knees to conform with Government regulations. The entry of 'hippies' and men with long hair and flared trousers is forbidden."

Like in much of Africa, every shop in Malawi had a photo of its leader, a smiling Banda, on its wall. When Banda visited a town, he expected to be greeted by dancing women.

Throughout much of his career, Everlasting worked as a bodyguard for Hastings Banda. For 25 or 26 years, he said, until 1987. Always armed with a pistol, Everlasting traveled ahead of the President sometimes, and sometimes he accompanied him. The President wore exotic three-piece suits, matching handkerchiefs and carried a fly-whisk.

"He was a man of contact and dialogue," Everlasting said with a smile. "He was a strong leader."

At the end of the road, the former advance man and bodyguard for the president, Everlasting Nyirenda happily accepted an unruly wad of kwacha with thanks as we parted ways at our ship, the MV Ilala, at Monkey Bay.

•••••

Less than the usual panoply of miscreants populated the MV Ilala, I thought. Approximately one, and then came three local fellows, Ben and Al and Al's cousin, who climbed aboard, before departure, just to have a look. The Ilala made itself available for tours at its port calls, and local folks were drawn to its mystique, I think, in the same way we used to go to the airport to watch the propeller planes take off whenever my dad was inside one of them.

A family of five, man, boys and a baby daughter, two of the sons in black suits and white shirts, their best clothes, were here just to stand along the dock and watch the commotion.

The MV Ilala is a tradition on Lake Malawi. It steams the length of the lake, three hundred miles, from Monkey Bay in the south to the Tanzanian border in the north and back again once a week, and has since 1951.

Seeing off the MV Ilala in their Sunday best.

We made the distinctly good choice of joining the Ilala in its home port, at Monkey Bay, where it docks for a good cleaning and a fresh crew. Some time later that cleanliness and order began to break down, and the beer ran out causing a morning switch to gin by the locals on board. That was dangerous. But by then it was time for us to go.

Just now we had the catbird's seat. Among the first aboard, we staked out more space than we were due on the second deck above the gangplank, in shade under a canvas awning. Our fellow passengers climbed aboard, but almost nobody came upstairs. The Africans, who came aboard carrying rugs and tubs and satchels, mostly traveled on the deck below, arrayed across rows of benches, in nooks and crannies.

"Oh those are just white people," Mirja tossed off as the occasional tourist like us came upstairs.

The Ilala was scheduled to set sail at 10:00. About 11:00 the Carlsbergs and Cokes arrived and blocked up the entryway as they loaded them in. Worth the wait. It was a late start with hot beers, and the big white coolers behind the bar never quite got them cold.

They had a little morale meeting, a pep talk for the employees out in the sun on the top deck. Four leaders addressed the crew, there was applause, then some unintelligible public address announcements, and at 11:30 we slipped our moorings.

The MV Ilala at Monkey Bay.

Nuts, salty peanuts and fish and sticky buns went on sale from plastic tubs.

Willis, the steward, was replacing the screen in our cabin's door. He'd done four round trips to the Tanzania end of Lake Malawi and back, and if he did this one and one more, he got two weeks off.

Up to now he was "passenger cook," stationed below, and now he'd been promoted to first class steward.

He went to find Panadol because by now Mirja, like so often after a long international flight, was poised for full health collapse. Her throat was crimson. We began to steal all the tissues in sight.

Shortly before noon they loosed a blast from the horn as we cleared the point at Zongo village at the end of Monkey Bay and moved into open water. It was Friday, and the Ilala would return to Monkey Bay on Wednesday.

The ticket takers came around, a team of three, smiling, thumbs up.

We cruised up the western shore.

Light showers danced occasionally along the deck. We sat up top in rattan seats near the Karonga Bar, where they made an attempt to keep the beer cold.

The first stop, after four hours, was to be the town of Chipoka.

Martin and his girlfriend, both young and Dutch, shared the port side of the deck with us. Martin was on a three-week holiday to see his girlfriend, a national park volunteer for four months.

I asked when she had to be back to work in the park and Martin just shrugged.

"She's a volunteer."

Their destination, Nkhata Bay, was one stop past where we were headed, Likoma Island.

And there was Katie, with her Peace Corps friend - Katie from Buffalo, four months into her two years, teaching forestry management techniques in neighboring Zambia.

Katie observed of Malawians, "They know how to use each other and not in an exploitive way. They make you family." A

Finnish doctor at Monkey Bay said that, too. She said her own baby ended up on local women's backs.

Big girls, Katie and her girlfriend were, in local wraps, hair on their legs, Katie reading a paperback by a female author, titled *Stiff*.

On the upper deck.

At the beginning they closed access to the upper deck when we were on the move. The folks downstairs had their own place for snacks and drinks. Martin and his girlfriend, the Peace Corps girls, another group of ripening young Europeans on the other side of the boat, and us, that was it.

It was a few days before Christmas and a deck hand played electrician behind the bar, trying to string up an elaborate array of Christmas lights. I lit a Café Crème and settled in with a Carlsberg. Two Carlsbergs were 160 kwacha, where 140 was a dollar. Mirja wrote postcards.

Willis, newly promoted and earnest steward, came around with a "menu" and we set lunch for 1:30: shredded beef, sima and piri piri. After he took orders around the deck, he came back with aspirin for Mirja.

Once out of Monkey Bay in open water, you could watch the showers, in little fits of a hundred meters wide, play out under cumulous clouds across the lake. If it weren't overcast, said Mirja, we'd be toast, and as it was, you didn't pour sweat but you did glisten.

We shared lunch with Steph and Tom from London, doing an epic ten months across Africa, northbound, hoping to make it to Addis overland, and then fly to Cairo.

They vehemently confirmed tales from Teija Kulmala, the Finnish doctor from back in Monkey Bay, of the twelve-hour ride from Lilongwe to Monkey Bay on the local bus, and they vowed never again to complain about London Transit.

Tom was a free-lance art director and Steph a teacher back home. They were stopping at Nhkota Bay for Steph to volunteer as a teacher. She taught sixth form at home (that's high school), and she hoped to teach primary school at Nhkota. Tom reckoned he'd be useless at teaching and so he hoped to maybe do some construction.

They were looking forward to structure, and after some time on the African road, they thought a job would be easier than the arduous business of travel by local means.

As they planned their itinerary across Tanzania to Kenya I spoke up for Zanzibar, the largely Muslim island a couple dozen miles off Dar Es Salaam, Tanzania, claiming the call to prayer as evocative. Tom replied that he often worked round the corner from Finsbury Park, home of the rabble-rousing North London Central Mosque, and that was all the evocative he needed.

•••••

Get Dirty for God. Go Lay a Brick with Team Mission. Thirty or forty kids wearing missionary T-shirts with those slogans came aboard to tour the Ilala at the first stop, Chipoka, from about 3:00 to 4:30.

A boy drew a crowd on the dock putting on a show with two bobble head monkeys on a table. Some people wore lime green sandals and others sold them.

If you ever sail the MV Ilala, choose the rattan seats to port, just above the gangplank, for live theatre immediately below you at port calls. The same seats are great when the port of call doesn't have a big enough dock for the Ilala to tie up. In that case an incredibly colorful, and incredibly crowded scrum scrambles onto and out of the tenders dispatched to shore. Just below you.

You learn to stake out your deck space. After that first stop, if you didn't, you'd lose it. The Ilala was vastly more crowded as soon as we left Chipoka.

Immanuel, deck hand, remarked on the Indian owners. I spoke later with Malcolm, the Indian commercial officer, who described Byzantine smuggling ruses he has seen.

In the evening a loud, rollicking, mostly European time broke out around the bar. We joined Richard, a kitchen outfitter, and his girlfriend from New York, the Aussie from Queensland who Mirja always thought was called John but who was named Peter, Martin the Dutch banker with a hankering for a posting to Southeast Asia, his girlfriend the park volunteer who was beginning to feel ill, and Steph and Tom.

We laid back in our cabin late in the morning, until the horn blew us standing and we were in Mozambique. That was at 9:00 and we didn't set sail again until after 11:00 because officials were involved, and procedures had to be followed.

We couldn't dock but instead anchored offshore and a flotilla of small craft commenced shuttling over and back to Ngoo, Mozambique.

We heard a splash, turned to see a body fly by the porthole and looked to see it was Tom and Peter the Aussie boy out for a swim. Good idea because it was hot hot hot in Mozambique, early in the morning.

Some Ilala crew predicted that the Mozambican customs men would try to charge Peter and Tom some money – make them buy an "entrance visa" for jumping into Mozambican water – but they never did.

Tenders shuttle passengers and freight to shore.

People washed clothes, tended fishing nets and did the things they do along the shore, the Ilala's two tenders shuttled over and back and I found a pitcher of boiled water down in the saloon for coffee. From shore, a little light, agreeable reggae gave it all a beachy feel.

We've been to Mali and Congo – Brazzaville if you count stopping at their airports, and according to Everlasting we have seen a goat in Mozambique. Now we were to spend days lurking just off the Mozambican coast, never quite making landfall.

Sign in the toilet:

"Navigation Hazard: Would passengers please ensure that curtains are drawn in cabin and bathroom before switching on lights after dark."

The PA announcer blew into the microphone first every single time he said anything. Ever.

Now, after two and a half hours of tenders shuttling, we pulled back from Mozambique, the breeze resumed with our motion and it was quiet and cool again.

Malawi lake flies swarmed to form clouds over the lake. Frightening. Locals told apocryphal stories of fishermen suffocating in their canoes after being caught in those swarms.

Peter the Aussie said people eat them. They swoop baskets through the swarms to catch them, then eat them fried and pressed into cakes.

Malawi lake flies.

Schoolteacher Francis Osward Manjanja, of the Mulunguzi Primary School in Blantyre, sat with us on deck. He drew a useful map of the route of the MV Ilala that explained how we'd left Monkey Bay, stopped at Chipoka and then in the middle of the night at Nkhotakota, then crossed the lake in darkness to stop, when the horn blasted us upright in the morning, at Mtengula, and then Ngoo, on the Mozambique side of Lake Malawi.

He said that while the good people of Ngoo live in Mozambique, they are Malawian and they use Malawian currency.

This was Francis's first trip on the Ilala, even though he'd lived in Blantyre since he was a boy of five. He'd brought his son and grandson.

Africans do not like to travel, he observed.

"We prefer to stay close to our families and learn of foreign lands and people from visitors. Like you," he smiled.

He ducked downstairs and brought back six anti-biotic Amoxicillin pills, a day's dose, and pain medication for Mirja, and once again disappeared onto the second class deck below, and though I looked for him, I never saw him again.

The Karonga Bar turned up radio coverage of a football match in a local language.

By lunchtime Mirja couldn't breathe, her throat was raw, she just didn't feel sociable and you couldn't blame her. Downstairs, I found another carafe of boiled water for a freeze-dried pack of chicken Saigon noodles we'd brought with us. Didn't need it from a hygiene point of view (which was the reason we'd brought it), but it allowed Mirja to eat in the cabin without getting dressed and then go back to bed.

The usual group of Europeans sat in the saloon talking about their dream vacations. Here we were in formerly deepest darkest Africa, and Steph was dreaming of a five star ski resort in the Alps. Africa weary? Perhaps just a tad.

While Mirja slept we enjoyed shredded beef again, by choice, and sima and fingers, or grits and okra. Just like back home in Georgia.

•••••

The Ilala ran out of beer at 3:00. They'd opened the bar at 6:00 a.m. and a crowd had stood drinking ever since. People crowded aboard at all the stops, and it hadn't taken long for the upstairs bar to be commandeered by a festive, thirsty local crowd.

The Europeans worried they'd turn to the hard stuff now and turn rowdy, since one group of three fellows had already had most of the bottle of brandy even before the beer was gone, and there'd be no restock of beer until Nkhota Bay the next day.

They felt they were covered, though, if they were discreet. An Austrian girl had eight bottles of Malawian Gin secretly stashed in the kitchen fridge, bought back in Monkey Bay because it was such a bargain, just $6 each.

Meanwhile the Dutch girl was down, head in Martin's lap, malaria suspected and, though they thought of heading on into Nkhata with the rest of the backpackers, they'd get off at Likoma Island, where there was a medical center where she could be tested. The boat arranged a car for her and would wait. Either they'd reboard, or not.

Anchored off Cobue village, Mozambique.

Six hours behind the timetable turned out to be a pretty good rule of thumb.

The main generators on Likoma Island had failed some days earlier and the government was scrambling to put that right.

The Ilala anchored off Cobue village, off Mozambique again, in mid-afternoon, and Likoma was visible a short distance, maybe a half hour steaming time away.

The day stretched on, the tenders scooted over and back, shadows lengthened and no lights came up on Likoma.

A positive scrum erupted when it came time to leave the Ilala at Likoma after dark. Truth was, we'd watched the same thing happen at all the other stops, but now we'd left our little cabin sanctuary behind and had to descend, clutching our bags, into the bananas and bodies and bolts of cloth.

Malcolm, the commercial officer, suggested that the boat from Kaya Mawa, our lodge, would likely come alongside, negating any need to go ashore on the Ilala's tenders, because Kaya Mawa was all the way around on the other side of Likoma Island. And so it did.

A man called James ushered us and four others aboard his motorboat and for the first time in days, as darkness surrounded us and the Ilala grew smaller, the main thing was the seductive, embracing quiet.

● ● ● ● ●

15 THE SOUTHERN CAUCASUS

The Wien Flughafen stood disturbingly deserted at night, all the shops stocked like Christmas, but you couldn't play with the toys. They glittered and blinked coquettishly behind glass doors pulled shut.

Our old buddy Austrian Airlines left Vienna on a beeline toward Budapest, then Timisoara, Bucharest, Constanta, over the Black Sea to Trabzon and on into Yerevan, all of it in blackness below. The flight tracking screen showed our destination tucked right in between Grozny and Baghdad: "Local time in Jerewan 4:31 a.m."

Austrian's corporate color scheme was brilliant red, the national color, and the cabin crew was dressed red hat to sensible (but red) shoes. Fetching, I thought.

Taxiing out ("We are number one for takeoff"), a wail arose behind us. A woman screamed "Go back, go back and check!" Crimson crew rushed to her and kneeled and huddled round our distraught Armenian. One of them came back forward and PA'd their apologies, "Dis is not Azerbaijan, ve know dis."

The safety announcements were recorded, and they were for the wrong destination. This woman wasn't by God going to Baku. Azerbaijan's border with Armenia had been shut tight for fifteen years.

All the Armenian men wore suits. Tomorrow was Whitsunday, "Something after Orthodox Easter," the lead flight attendant explained, "You know, about when Jesus goes up in the air...."

It might still have been the Soviet era but for all the smiles at the otherwise wholly Soviet Zvarnots airport. They still wore the huge Russian era Hats of Officialdom. As Levon, our man in Armenia, went to fetch his Volga sedan we shuddered at the concrete monstrosity of an airport the Soviet Union had imposed on its Armenian Republic.

Out on the road Levon swept his hands expansively. "Las Vegas of Armenia," he said as we rolled through a garish land of neon casinos, empty but lit at 5:00 a.m. The very faintest hint of a brightening horizon gathered below Mars and we headed through deserted streets, over trolley tracks without the trolleys and through deserted traffic circles.

Wide boulevards stood utterly dark under streetlights, not a single one lit. Benzene stations and shops with indeterminate wares were lit by multi-colored neon and looked architecturally like maybe the Dari-Dip in the 1960s back home.

A vague scent of damp fires, cheap coal and urine evoked memories of the distinct smell of Soviet Russia. After the sign marking the end of Yerevan (the word Yerevan with a line through it, the way they do), a chill settled over the fields and we cruised down a serviceable four lane split highway to Khor Virap Monastery, about 30 kilometers south of town. It was closed when we arrived.

We served ourselves up as breakfast for mobs of mosquitoes. Levon made us understand that the fourth parallel road out that way was in Turkiye, as was Mt. Ararat, which towered beyond. A really big statue on a hill, Georg somebody, Armenian partisan, stands and taunts the Turks still. Levon explained that ahead on this road was Nagorny Karabakh. He used "Nagorny" (meaning "highland"), while we always hear the Soviet era name "Nagorno" at home.

Khor Virap and Mt. Ararat at dawn.

When they realized they had guests, the Khor Virap caretakers agreeably opened up and let us poke around the main building, which dates from the 1600s, like everything else seems to between the Caspian and Black Seas. The guy with the key walked around in sort of Mediterranean shirttails-out fashion and the other fellow mainly sported a massive mustache.

Levon pointed at a smokestack and told us, "Cement factory." I may have gotten him all wrong, but he seemed to take pride in explaining, waving his finger and emphasizing, TWO cement factories! Could it be there are only two cement factories in Armenia, and that even so this is a source of pride?

Levon would later drive us to Tbilisi (Tiflis to him), so we got to know Levon's Volga. It was black inside, with a Blaupunkt cassette player, a picture of virgin and Son on the dash and a pair of miniature boxing gloves hanging from a visor. A ding on the windshield caused the view to warp precisely at eye level.

Levon himself was very fair in a world of dark Armenians, and well turned out, in a gray jacket, checked white shirt and black slacks. With his ready smile, you felt you could trust him.

And the landscape, sun up now, felt comfy too, spread out, with long sight lines, hills gently rising into the far distance, backed in one or two directions by snowy mountains. People worked the fields as the sun rose. Four car doors were strung together to make a gate across a lane through a field.

Straight ahead ten miles down the A325 highway Armenia, Turkey and Azeri-held Nakhichevan met, and another six miles down the road was the border with Iran, but it wasn't a landscape you'd associate with Iran. Fields of just emerging low yellow crops, perhaps rape, stretched among tall cedars and slender poplars.

The common folk sold petrol from soft drink bottles on tables by the road. One lady sold flowers, too. Flowers and petrol.

The good people of Armenia are close to the earth. Farmers, just the shapes of them really, moved toward the fields, rakes, hoes and scythes over their shoulders. Three heaping baskets of strawberries filled the back of an orange Lada ahead of us as we rolled into Yerevan.

Yerevan streets were rife with remnants. Leftover communism, not their fault but their reality: remnant autos, housing and attitudes. Used Ladas and Zighulis and Volgas. Not as much nouveau flash as contemporary Russia. Lots more like Russia than the U.S.

Couples aging and young alike sat under trees and flirted. Men without shirts mowed a forlorn park. Mashtots Avenue was busy with traffic and shops and change booths, and young people with their phones.

If you were young in Yerevan you had a cell phone. The telephony infrastructure was so decrepit it behooved to erect towers. The girls wore tight pants. Unfortunately what passed for male fashion was still the black-with-trim, mafia-and-running-suit look that used to be the rage in post-Soviet Russia.

Newlyweds, preceded by a car video-taping their antics, stood through the sunroof in their limousine, as they took a few spins around Republic Square in the center of the capital.

The Foreign Ministry on Republic Square, Yerevan.

At an outdoor café associated with the Palace of Culture a half block off the square, a former Peace Corps volunteer remarked how Armenia had grown sharply more European in his five year absence.

We had business at the Sati Travel Agency, where a manager named Noune sat us down for remarks. She kept pulling a shock of gray back into her black hair.

She told us about her sons, in photos on a table behind her. This one was in Boston! A medical student! The other? Oh, he lived in Moscow. She was dismissive. He was in television.

Noune was only some months into her job. She had been a concert violinist but finally resigned herself to the need to get paid. She complained, "Our only pension is ten, fifteen dollars a month. Electricity is expensive, sometimes more than one hundred, but some people make less than one hundred."

"In the U.S. I know, you can make five thousand, ten thousand dollars in a month, it is depending on what you do, but here? Maybe two hundred."

That's a big difference. There's also a difference in what she says Armenians expect from their leaders.

"We take care of each other, we can not expect the government to."

•••••

Blood feuds have plagued the Caucasus for centuries. Some clans in Chechnya have been at war for so long they don't remember the incident that provoked the vendetta. And here, I think, Noune put her finger on where blood feuds and honor killings become the least bit more conceivable.

Civil society was a wreck in the post-Soviet periphery. Outside Russia everybody made the best of their battered Russian remnants, and in remote places beyond Soviet penetration, civil society never existed, and sometimes still doesn't. Ruling the village was divided among clans, who made and enforced the laws, such as they were.

Jason Burke wrote about blood feuds in his book *On the Road to Kandahar*: "Such ritualized and overt violence ... publicly demonstrated the power of a ... tribe to chastise those who transgress its rules...." And it may help, somehow, to push back at a hostile, encroaching world.

There was no fighting here in Armenia. Noune stoutly asserted this, dismissing any other possibility.

No, it was not a war, this conflict that raged both before and after the Soviet collapse, and that displaced maybe a million Armenians and Azeris, centered around the small Armenian enclave of Nagorno-Karabakh. Noune explained that it all happened because of the great earthquake of 1988, after which the good people of Nagorno-Karabakh rose up and demanded places to live, which was their right.

A man in this office went to fight, she told us.

"He is great patriot. And may I say," she said, with a thin smile, "Very heartbroken."

So the Armenia/Azerbaijan standoff wasn't going Armenia's way. But what was?

•••••

Noune's office charged my Visa card 40,000 Manats eight times because they didn't know how to charge more than 40,000 at once. They had only had a Visa terminal since April, and they said they were the first travel agent in town to get one.

Just before the last charge went through the receipt roll ran out, and a long wait ensued as staff, I guess, ran around town to find more paper. Finally we all agreed a photocopy for each of us would be just as good.

So we rolled out of Yerevan. But in the suburbs they called Levon to come back. Noune stood on the street with a form she forgot for us to sign attesting to the services they'd rendered, because I guess all hell would descend on Sati Travel if they made money and the government didn't know about it.

It was just as well we came back. We forgot water, so I went to get some and Noune followed me. She spoke a few words to the vendor and he handed me two bottles and waved my money away.

"We help each other."

And later, when we ate lunch at Lake Sevan, they wouldn't take our money for Levon. We paid, Levon ate free.

He brings you to our restaurant. We help each other.

•••••

Leaving Yerevan you'll see a cloister, the zoo, a big water park with curvy slides, the statue to Mashtots (Saint Mesrop Mashtots, inventor of the Armenian alphabet, born around 360) and the engineering and medical institutes.

Yerevan is bigger than Podgorica, Montenegro, capital of the last former Yugoslav state to declare itself independent, but the two have a lot in common. Leafy and dry, battered and saddled with making do with post-communist remains, and never meant to be a national capital. If you live in either place, I imagine it's a slow but altogether agreeable, family-based way of life.

Huge new housing blocks rose from the hills outside Yerevan, mostly unfinished. Levon made a sign with his hands. "Communist," he said, and showed this much. "Now," he indicated much less.

He made a motion with his hand like something falling off a table, like, 'End of Communism, end of dachas.' Sometimes there were whole hillsides of sandy-colored unfinished housing.

Noune said Armenians from Iran were trying to move to Armenia because the government in Iran is terrible.

"Of course it's okay, they're Armenian!"

•••••

Lavender & yellow wild flowers bloomed and temperatures cooled outside the valley around Yerevan. White bushes bloomed in the median of the M4. Tired brown evergreens slumped down slopes in lumpy, listless contrast to a bright yellow soil. With altitude, snowy patches appeared on the hillsides, in summer retreat.

Lake Sevan boasted a proliferation of straw hat and beach towel stands. All around the lake makeshift shashlik grills stood, usually unattended.

Ka – Ra – Ma, Levon chanted at a place. Ka – Ra – Ma. Karama had spotty snow here and there in the fields. Levon gestured to a village over on the left and told us, "Yuri Gegarin," the Soviet cosmonaut, the first man in orbit in 1961.

A car park led to a walk up to the Lake Sevan monastery. Men sang traditional songs or played stringed instruments for tips, and quit immediately as you walked past.

Welcome to Lake Sevan.

They barbecued fish at a terrace restaurant laid out against deep blue water. Reminded me just the least bit of Lake Baikal, not Lake Sevan itself, but the surroundings - old Russian trucks, unkempt landscaping and signs in Cyrillic. But families were enjoying their day in the sun, there were jet skis out on the water and the lake was busy sprouting resort hotels.

Lake Sevan is remarkable. At 1900 meters (6200 feet), it's the world's highest alpine lake. That explained the snow fields in June.

From a delicate salad of dill, flat leaf parsley and tiny green onions, Levon picked a few pieces, folded them back on each other a couple of times so that they fit onto a torn piece of lavash and rolled the bread into a roll around them.

He grinned and said, "Armenian sandwich."

Then, beaming, he did the same with a slice of cheese, "Armenian sandwich – anything!"

We watched a bus's exhaust start a brush fire in the parking lot. We were way above it. Boys, just two of them, came with bowls of water and rags to put it out.

At intervals on the road past the lake, men stood outside shipping containers by the roadway. They walked toward the Volga as we approached and pointed the index fingers of both hands at the car, arms held a certain distance apart. They were selling fresh lake fish, advertising them as, "this big."

Rusty 1960's vintage buses plied the roads. Forested villages scrolled by one after the next, stone houses tucked under outcrops of rock, dramatic vertical relief, not many cars, most people on foot. Most wore straw hats against the sun, lending a sense of languor.

Few material goods, but of course fashion (or its impostor) imposed itself. A girl on a street corner wore a t-shirt with the English words "Love Team M."

We'd doze, and Levon, trying his endearing best to be tour guide without a common language, would declaim something like, "Gomarodie!" and grin and poke the air with his finger and show us five or six teeth. A sign announced, "Pambak." In Pambak you could buy Byuregh distilled water.

Top-heavy Kamaz trucks struggled up switchbacks in smoke-choked queues while we glided down. Breezy cool, it was a brilliant afternoon, the moon waxing through half full, high in the sky at five in the afternoon.

Through the pine forests of Lori we ran inside a narrow defile along the Debed River, which crashed through the center of Dzoraget town where men fished on rocks. It was one of those places where the water has carved so far down into the valley that the sun must leave the valley floor by noon.

They were having a go at making Dzoraget a holiday village, with a fancy hotel called the Avan, featured in Travel & Leisure magazine on a page called "Where to go next." It must have had some earlier heyday, because there were remnants of cable cars long rusted to a stop. On a few buildings they were replacing cement walls with new siding.

You couldn't leave Armenia without one last monastery, called Sanahin, from 996 in the reign of Ashot the Bagratuni (doesn't he sound like a comic book hero?), a time when fortresses and not borders marked the extent of rule. It was perched so high on a hill that even the thought of hauling the building stones up there was crippling.

Ashot the Bagratuni was an enlightened ruler. His fortress housed a school of higher education and a library.

Levon, bless him, would be seriously late by the time he got us to Tbilisi and turned around to head back home, but he dutifully and without reluctance offered to take us up there, and he didn't even show relief when we declined.

The road north to Georgia.

Now we settled into gliding around curves and following stream or canyon rim until gradually the hills were lower and the vegetation shrank from alpine to more scrub than trees, and it was hot again. Cows walked the roads untended.

When we stopped to fill up, Levon smiled and declared, "Toilet is Europe NO!"

They dispensed petrol into a tank in the trunk, and everybody smoked. Mirja and I scrambled out of the car to avoid what looked like an inferno to come. A young man called out to me. I had no idea what he was saying of course, and Levon said something that caused him to laugh and rush over to shake my hand.

"Good morning I am David," he smiled, even though it was late afternoon.

"Good morning I am Bill," I replied as we embraced.

Levon told me David was alarmed at my camera and thought I must be the police.

On the Armenian side of the border the officials were indifferent. It was stifling and still. Georgia customs was a shipping container with peeling green paint. They'd made a go at an awning to provide a little shade but it was long gone, its supports rusted away, and three boys, one in uniform, smoked and stared ahead. We did the simple formalities with a Georgian official in approximate French and it all came off with no baksheesh.

In Georgia, sheep and the smell of wood smoke. Craggy, naked hills. For miles people trod the roadside, and there was simply no commerce.

Giant cedars demarked fields, the roads were pocked and potholed, and there was much more holdover Cyrillic than in Armenia. And then there was this comically giant traffic circle, pertinent to nothing.

A vast plain opened before us, and way, way over on the other side stood some kind of fortress or monument on a hill. We made our way toward it. The air was fragrant and a lake spread far below on the right. We descended to merge with a highway in the valley, and ran straight up on the fortress. Predictably, it was a monastery. It held a sweeping view of the next valley floor – and Tbilisi.

•••••

The Marriott Tbilisi offered an island of luxury, and we took them up on it. Eventually we strolled along main street, Rustaveli Boulevard, down toward the massive old Soviet telephone and telegraph building at the far end of the street. From there we followed a warren of cobbled streets down to the river Mtkvari.

On the way pensioners sold family artifacts and whatever else they'd got their hands on, old swords and telephone parts, cutlery and cigarettes, all spread out on mats on the sidewalks, below the leafy canopy of a park.

The sign on the first building across the river was in Georgian, an indecipherable, squiggly script. This was a restaurant, and we went inside.

Sometime in Greek antiquity Jason and his Argonauts sailed safely through the Symplegades, rocks that crushed anything that tried to pass between them, to land in Colchis, the Black Sea coast of present day Georgia. After performing a series of heroic tasks, Jason seized the object of his quest, the Golden Fleece.

In honor of the Argonauts we enjoyed cold Argo beers among men at wooden tables drinking beer and eating khinkali, the Georgian equivalent of pelmeni, Russian meat pastries. Three men in costume wandered out of the back, sat on low chairs in front of a hearth and played the traditional Caucasian reed instrument, the duduki.

An old man in a bright orange jumpsuit with BP on its breast took our picture from a table across the room, so we took his too. He grinned, got up and left, and came back with ice cream bars for Mirja and me. He showed us his pictures and said something like, "Souvenir for me, gift for you."

•••••

Before we left the U.S. we arranged for a man named Zaza to drive us up the Georgia Military Highway into the high Caucasus. Trouble was, he couldn't be reached. All day long we tried his cell phone and it rang busy.

Turned out Zaza's cell phone number required that you press "8" first, but then we got an intercept message that said try again later. I called all night and the next morning, right past our planned departure time.

Finally he answered. Zaza's voice was deep, his accent thick. I gathered, I'm not sure how, that he'd let the driver go because we hadn't called, but that he'd do some scrambling, and we set a rendezvous for noon.

We waited in the lobby until long after twelve. I called from the lobby, he answered and I saw him there, outside the hotel, talking to me through the glass. He was walking up and down the sidewalk wondering where the hell we were. We got our things stuffed into the trunk of an aging Volga sedan, perched on the springy back seat and we were off for Kazbegi, up by the Russian border.

Not until we stopped for several monasteries, of course, the first at the ancient Georgian capital of Mtskheta, at the picture-perfect meeting of the Mtkvari and Aragvi Rivers, where Saint Nino brought Christianity east from Cappadocia in the fourth century. Still today Nino is a popular name for Georgian girls.

These monasteries marked the founding of the Georgian nation, one on a hill overlooking town, and another in the town center, where Zaza explained the ins and outs of the founding of Georgia, all the while crossing himself and kissing this or that holy object. Kings were buried there.

The Mtkvari and Aragvi Rivers.

•••••

Georgian toasts are famous, arduous and daunting, with a well-developed ritual. Zaza ordered a remarkably large pitcher of wine along with our beers (Zviadi, our driver, was stoic with his coffee). We're never gonna down that thing, I thought. But we did.

Zaza's toasts were masterful little journeys backward to where he wanted to be. He started out with "Now I would like to toast to one man..." and ended up with a salute to the traveling spirit.

"Even little things have a beauty," he began again, and did a little riff on "be here now."

A sort of cheese pizza called khachapuri was just stunningly good. The 'pickle,' an array of cucumbers, tomatoes, red onions and a salad, like in Armenia, came as a plate trimmed with green onions, flat-leaf parsley and dill.

There were kebabs and beans and fungus, greens that tasted vaguely like licorice, stuffed baby aubergines, a beef salad and a deep dish of fried cheese, yet more bread, a sauce called Satsivi to go with barbecued meat, more salad with thyme sprigs, lemonade, several more beers and many more toasts.

The Georgian toast is a circumlocutionary art:

"All good history is continuous" evolved into a toast to friendship.

A really poignant toast, I thought, started out "Every moment is the present" and ended up being "to people who are at home worrying about us."

It may be the savior of the Georgian soul, or at least its work ethic, that Georgian wine is mild, and doesn't object to being gulped. We drank and he toasted and he toasted and we drank and ate, until lunch hit the two hour mark and we were scarcely outside Tbilisi, the Georgian Military Highway was still a theory, and by now it was mid-afternoon.

Still more toasts as we lingered, and finally, with a lofty start, Zaza began the parting toast "To safe journey," which ended more earthily, with a smile and the assurance that once we're in Kazbegi, "Then again we can drink."

When President Putin banned Georgian wine, bottled water and produce, the pretense was that they didn't meet basic health standards. It was a political irritant for Georgia, nothing more, but for the record, this particular Georgian wine left us feeling considerably more healthy as we got up to leave.

Three and a half hours after leaving Tbilisi and just fifteen kilometers outside town, we hit the open road, mountains beckoning, traffic light, in the direction of the border, our destination ten kilometers from Chechnya.

Leaving Mtskheta, like coming in, involved a comical set of looping highway circles, on this side of the main road then that, as if gaining momentum for the launch up onto the Georgia Military Highway, the traditional route across the high Caucasus used to pillage and trade through the ages.

Mirja and I bounced up and down on the back seat of Zviadi's Volga. Zaza mostly fit in the front seat, scooting to one side to fit his knees up against the dash. Most of this Volga's dashboard appeared not to have worked for years, the Yamaha cassette player included.

Zaza was all decked out in denim, with a silly Putin grin and a crumpled sailor's cap he wore against the sun. Zviadi, after his coffee, was dark and intense, and an unrelenting smokestack. He was much younger than the rest of us and spoke no English at all. He crossed himself like a madman, repeatedly, time after time, as we drove past any kind of religious symbol, and there were many.

Old women sold ice cream and cigarettes on the highway, leaning back against the center divider. The same round orange buses as in Armenia plied Georgian highways. And of course the road wasn't that good for very long.

But never was the sun more brilliant, the air more crisp, and the light, somehow, had a northern latitude clarity. In time the mountains of the high Caucasus, blue in afternoon haze, stacked up three, then four deep.

Vladikavkaz is the capital of the Russian republic of Ingushetia, just west of Chechnya, and the Georgian Military Highway continues to there. In time the notion of "highway" became a memory, and at 4:30 we found ourselves at a sign reading "Gudari 68, Vladikavkaz 141."

Perfect snow-capped cones and pointy peaks filled the horizon, and then a jagged one, low in the crook of the near ones. We stopped to peer over a precipice – the verge of a steep defile, at 2395 meters, in intermittent ice fields, with streams and more lavender and yellow flowers.

Up to the border with Ingushetia, the last 36 kilometers were the de rigueur final endurance run. And straight from the screenplay, rain splattered the windshield, kicking up a muddy film the Volga's vestigial wipers only smeared.

•••••

Each end of Kazbegi's main square comprised nothing much, with a road wandering off each way, one in the direction from which we'd come, from Tbilisi, the other to Vladikavkaz. A hotel sat on one side and on the fourth side, opposite the hotel, a half dozen kiosks all sold the same things, the petty little consumer goods necessary for life. All had tissues and matches and drinks, but not cold. There wasn't refrigeration anywhere in the whole lot.

The wares on offer took up all the window space, so the salespeople sat back invisible and desultory behind a little open window in the middle. You wouldn't call these kiosk capitalists sullen. Crestfallen might be the better word.

Kazbegi itself rose on a low hill behind the kiosks. A walk among the houses revealed bright flowers on windowsills and smoking men seated on low benches with a wary eye and a suspicious nod of the head to a stranger. No traffic. Massive amounts of trash were cast onto the ground, pigs snuffling through it. A dump truck-sized Kamaz lumbered by, an unlikely family vehicle that deposited a scarf-clad old woman with a basket down at the bottom of the hill.

At any particular time, six or eight or ten old Russian-made cars congregated at the center of the square, their drivers in little knots smoking and waiting for the odd passenger to here or there. Zaza hired a red Lada Niva, strong with a high undercarriage. Just the right vehicle to haul us up to the Holy Trinity church, way up the hill. We'd drive up and walk down.

Little streams ran right down the middle of the road.

From above, Kazbegi looked pleasant and cleaner than it was. You couldn't see all the trash in the fast-moving River Terek. They reckoned that it was all being swept away to Russia, so what did it matter?

Way at the back of town stood a huge block building. They always used to call those places "sanatoriums" in Soviet days. Zaza said that in the old days 300 tourists came here from all over the Soviet Union every day.

That was all gone now. Zaza had been reading what the Russians were saying about Georgians in internet chat rooms, and it was "Not fantastic, more than fantastic. They are saying we will eat them if they come."

Hiking the high Caucasus.

By my count we represented a tourism trickle of exactly four people staying in the Stepantsminda hotel's forty-odd rooms, Mirja and me, Zaza and one other American.

The mountains behind Kazbegi town rose jagged and spectacular, holding their winter snow into June. Mt. Blanc, the highest place in the Alps, is 4807 meters. Mt. Kazbeg stood taller than all the Alps at 5033 meters, making its own weather, its snow-clad summit spinning off clouds, its glacier visible, massive, powerful.

•••••

When the Gergeti Holy Trinity Church was built, it was surrounded by a village, since disappeared, called Gergeti, whose inhabitants held the mandatory role of serfs to and caretakers of the church and its surrounds. At that time it marked the northernmost point in Georgia.

The founding legend had it that three contending kings argued about in whose jurisdiction the church should be. A village elder in Mtskheta proposed to slaughter a dry cow (not a valuable milk-giving one) and cast one of its bones out to the edge of the village. A raven would take the bone, and where it stopped they'd build the church. They followed the raven to Ananuri, where they erected a cross, and then here to Gergeti.

Oxen delivered building stones for the church from villages fifteen kilometers away, and spring water for the masons came by sheep. Today that spring is called "Kalata," or mason.

The Gergeti Holy Trinity Church.

There was a service in progress as we arrived, but no evidence of a congregation. Someone called His Grace Stepantsminda and Khevi Bishop Peter "rather often" performed liturgies at the Holy Trinity Church, and even farther up at the highest place among all Orthodox churches, 4200 meters, at an icy little outpost they call Glacier Holy Trinity Church.

We didn't disturb the service but we did disturb a young man with bright red tennis shoes, who was offended by the beers Zaza hauled up for us, so we retreated outside the church grounds and enjoyed warm sunshine and a stiff wind, gazing out on the scenery with lunch of beer and potato snacks.

The walk back down to Kazbegi town wound through low canopied birch forest. Birch trees are my favorite. Tall and majestic or young and strong, in stands or solo, birches always look clean and prim, never straggly and hang-down like some of their tropical cousins.

They hold their leaves, which are too small for the trunk, tightly to their sides. The collective sound of birch leaves rattling in wind isn't a loping, lazy wave, but more of a busy flutter that collectively comes 'round to the sound you make when you slide into a bed of freshly washed linens.

It took an hour's walk to reach the uppermost settlements, poor stone houses close together, not many people on the streets at midday, and the thick, stifling smell of pigs. Once again a little stream sometimes appeared in the middle of the road. A shipping container stood along the road, locked, its curtains half pulled shut. "Kebabi," read a sign on the front.

A woman in boots walked slowly up the hill. A man, maybe crazy, laughed and danced and pulled water from a stream into a big bucket. Two boys, one with a long switch, walked toward a herd of cows in the fields. The sound of rushing water from the Terek walked with you everywhere.

•••••

The Hotel Stepantsminda was owned by the brewers of Kazbegi beer, one of the two top Georgian brands (along with Argo). Its common rooms were always dark and empty, its front door locked at night with the key left in the lock. There was no one behind the reception desk. There were no lifts, and four floors with ten rooms each.

Room 21 had two low double beds and a Fujeta brand TV showing channels Rustav 1 & 2. On Rustav 1: A crime show, a sitcom, a show with singing and pianos, and a soap opera starring, best I could tell, King Hussein of Jordan (or his twin). Rustavi 2 wasn't on the air most of the time. The hot water worked, a fine asset in raw mountain air.

The dining room downstairs opened onto a terrace with aluminum tables and chairs over the Terek. Occasional showers raked the terrace. It was almost always cold. But sun would return and dry everything quickly, and it was bracing to sit outside and enjoy the stiff wind down the river valley.

Menus were fixed. Breakfast of hot bread, fish and boiled eggs, coffee and tea with lemons started at nine. Before nine, one morning there was a coffee pot with mugs that read "Maldun Seramik," and another morning there was nothing.

Breakfast and dinner were served on little wooden tables with red tablecloths and hard backed wooden chairs.

Grainy black and white photos from the early twentieth century hung all along the walls. One, called "Karnaval at Kazbegi," from 1926, showed several dozen people frozen transfixed by the camera, the way they stood back in those days, all wearing their various ethnic headgear, a man holding a cross dressed all in white, men with rifles and swords, kids in tunics, military men, two women in elaborate headdresses and one unfortunate dullard frozen in rigid salute, facing the wrong way.

Our fellow guest at the Stepantsminda was Chris Adam from Raleigh, North Carolina. Chris was dark and slight, well conditioned, and wore the look of a man who had been here too long. He had a driver and a personal translator. He was here to build the U.S. Army Corps of Engineers border post with Russia, a few miles up the road beside the river.

We drove out to see his project. Inside his office, a metal shed, blueprints foresaw a modern outpost of civilization right here on this spot, unlike anything vaguely in actual evidence. Chris's driver sat inside, a hairy Georgian who was always on his cell phone. He sat over a laptop and I asked, astonished, if they had the internet out here and he smiled, no, it was movies.

One month later the border, the only proper border between Russia and Georgia, was closed. After a week of back and forth provocations in Russian-occupied South Ossetia, the Russians closed it with two hours notice on the pretext that their side needed "repair work."

We were back home by then, but Chris emailed gamely, "Now I do not need to worry about vehicle and pedestrian traffic." Not that that was the whole point of the project, or anything.

The Georgia/Russian border post, pending.

•••••

The ride in from Georgia foreshadowed what Azerbaijan was all about. In the morning, the train windows filled with oil derricks and post-Soviet housing.

It had been entertaining the night before, rolling out of Tbilisi, to talk with young Georgian businessmen who were certain that in any Middle East, or, for that matter, any other war, Georgia would be victim to summary Russian bombing for its petulant courtship of NATO.

Now, for breakfast, they served coffee, bread and individually wrapped cheese slices, which were cut in half to appear to be more.

The improbably named Viking train consisted of the engine, two sleeping cars and a restaurant car in between, and was priced far outside local means. The price of admission apparently bought express service at the border. Zaza had rued our having to deal with the border, but he had only traveled the local train, which spent, he said, some hours on each side. In our case, we surrendered our passports on boarding, crossed into Azerbaijan in the restaurant car and that was it.

•••••

They would have you understand that Baku is crawling with western oilmen. Besides the Hyatt, where harried, uneasy young guys in ill-fitting suits rode elevators to meeting rooms, we found neither Texans nor cowboy hats. In fact, Baku, of the three South Caucasus capitals, easily filled the bill as the most Soviet city, with a bonus – head scarves.

Down at the waterfront the Maiden Tower (originally dating from the eleventh century, with an inside-the-fortress well) had a fine view of the old town and the harbor and a ferris wheel enclosed in a strip of trees.

A concrete bund stretched down the Caspian Sea waterfront, waves were in full chop, and families promenaded. Beside an amusement park full of kids and moms, you could enjoy Efes beers from Turkey under shade trees in the fine sea breeze.

Baku was a company town. Oil wealth provided for a fine mix of ethnic restaurants. It had built an urbane and modern pedestrian plaza called "Traders Street," reminiscent of Baku's glory days. In the 1890's, Baku pumped half the world's oil supply and Europe's finest architects clambered to build signature buildings. Stay close to Trader's Street and you're in Europe. Head out of town, though, and it's a little different.

•••••

Baku from the Maiden Tower.

April, 2006: The arriving guests filed into the Gulustan palace between double rows of male and female dancers clothed in national dress. The hall was decked out with roses and orchids delivered from the Netherlands. Proclamations were read from presidents Bush and Putin, to a crowd that included the Prime Minister, the Speaker and the heads of the ministries of Foreign Affairs, National Security, Emergency Situations, Culture, Economic Development and Health Protection, and the Mayor of Baku.

The Moscow guests included well-known couturiers, a composer, a humorist and other entertainers, notable for their extravagant dress. National cuisine was presented at the wedding, to which guests were warned in advance not to take photo or video cameras or cell phones. Instead the entire event was recorded by the "personal shooting team" of the Azerbaijani president, and by NTV Russia.

The bride and groom left the hall at 2:00 a.m. Two weeks later Leyla and Emin would celebrate their wedding in Moscow.

Leyla was Azerbaijani President Ilham Aliyev's "senior daughter," and Emin Agalarov was the son of Moscow developer Aras Agalarov, heir to his $730 million fortune. He fancied himself something of a popular singer.

And now we sat in the back of Rashad's Lada sedan listening to "Still," a sort of spoken-word song by Emin. Rashad had downloaded "Still" from the internet (he gave me a 'Where else, stupid?' kind of look) and was acting proud to have it.

We hired Rashad and his Lada to drive us out to a derelict drilling island called Artyom, both a world away from and the very reason for Baku's busy oil-driven affluence.

•••••

Rashad, in slacks, fashionable shades and a red T-shirt, didn't pay much attention to politics. He could tell, though, by a posse of cops in the road, that President Aliyev would be coming in past us from his country place, and sure enough, his motorcade swept past.

Maybe Rashad knew this because his family had a summer place near the president. His father had been, he told us, a mushroom farmer, but that business was done.

Once Rashad drove with a friend to Germany. They bought a Mercedes and drove it back and sold it. They didn't make much money because they had a great time on the way back, but they enjoyed the hell out of it.

•••••

The drilling towers, in groups of twos and threes mostly long abandoned, cast skeletal shadows on the scrub and brown of the earth, on pools of oil or grease. Heavy metal poles jutted from the ground, all canted at odd angles, and if they were longer they would have converged. Maybe these were drilling masts begun but abandoned, or maybe they had fallen or been dismantled, and the rest of them had been carried off.

Along the causeway that connected the Abseron peninsula to the island of Artyom (now renamed Pirallahi), an abandoned drilling mast stood alongside the broken bases of others, their rusty remains in the water beside them.

A man stopped his car. His passenger climbed out and glared at us as I took pictures of the gloom. Oil spread in shallow pools, and it wasn't clear if it was there through neglect or if it rose spontaneously from the earth.

The remains of concrete buildings had crumbled to expose rebar. A few of the "nodding donkeys" were still slowly pumping in spite of being rusted brown through and through, and the entire enterprise stretched nearly as far as the eye could see. Some drilling rigs were tied down with guy wires, and they combined with high tension power lines to describe a crazy random etching across the haze, itself merely a lighter shade of the oily blue-brown earth.

Artyom Island, Azerbaijan.

When a bore hole doesn't produce adequately, one way to get more oil is to employ a submersible pump. Wherever a nodding donkey still slowly raised and lowered its head, a power line ran to a pump, with a transformer on a pole tied to it in the crudest way.

There was a salt pan lined with household trash, maybe because of tidal action. Two rough green trucks lumbered through the mess; One looked implausibly like a logging truck, with big metal brackets at the front and back. The truck following held a pumping device on its flat bed. The left of the bed was jacked up way higher, so that the whole rear slanted awkwardly down to the right. It had six brand new, formidably-treaded tires.

People lived in two places on the island, at the village of Artyom at the northern tip, and at Ostrov Artema, a collection of block housing. Here an old round bus gasped for air at the curb. It was blue and white, with blue curtains pulled completely shut in each of the four windows along the side. All the windows were surrounded with corrosion, and streaks of dried rust ran down the bus from the bottom of each window.

A low fence surrounded a tin-roofed building that looked, improbably, to be somebody's house. Pipes ran along the salt pans and the road, and off the island along the causeway.

Leaving Artyom a sign, paint peeling, quoted former president (the current president's father) Heydar Aliyev: "Oil Is Our Treasure, and Azerbaijan's Future Is Bright Through Oil."

•••••

Baku is a contraction of its ancient name, Badu Kuba, or city of winds. All our time in Baku, its best feature was a stiff, unrelenting wind off the Caspian Sea, that sent up a hard chop offshore every single day. Several dozen photos I took out there at Artyom were blurred worthless by the wind.

•••••

What's right in strongman states like Azerbaijan is that your flight departs precisely, to the minute, on time. And we did. What's wrong in places like Azerbaijan is sullen, petty officialdom. The Heydar Aliyev airport gleamed bright and new in the predawn, welcoming from the outside, way out from town, but inside it already looked old in the Soviet way, low ceilings, loitering thugs (at 3:00 in the morning) and needless levels of unsmiling functionnaires.

I had been dubious about the cult of the Aliyevs, about how a leadership cult would work in this day and age. But from appearances it was real, with the Great Leader's pronouncements posted on billboards along the roadside, and with Rashad's general endorsement.

Rising from the Aliyev airport to the east we just nipped the Caspian shore. Venus hung bright and low as the eastern horizon pinked up, though we fled it. We banked to face Odessa, then Vienna.

The wisdom of Heydar Aliyev.

•••••

ABOUT THE AUTHOR

Bill Murray first ventured outside the United States to Montreal in 1980. Since then he's traveled to over a hundred countries and territories from Albania to Zimbabwe, mostly with his wife Mirja. They've taken three round-the-world trips.

Mirja and Bill live on a horse farm in the southern Appalachian mountains of Georgia, USA.

● ● ● ● ●

To see all the photos in this book in color, more photos corresponding to each chapter, and additional commentary, go to *A Common Sense and Whiskey Companion* at:

www.EarthPhotos.com/CSandW

CPSIA information can be obtained at www.ICGtesting.com
Printed in the USA
238159LV00006B/73/P